# Food for Thought

# Food for Thought

How Our Dollar Democracy Drove 2 Million
Canadians into Foodbanks to Collect Private
Charity in Place of Public Justice

## Marlene Webber

Coach House Press
Toronto

Published with the assistance of the Canada Council, the Ontario Arts Council and the Ontario Ministry of Culture and Communications.

Editor for the Press: David McFadden
Cover Design: Christopher Wadsworth / Reactor
Cover Photo: Ralph Bower. Used by permission of the *Vancouver Sun*.
Printed in Canada

Coach House Press
401 (rear) Huron Street
Toronto, Canada
M5S 2G5

Canadian Cataloguing in Publication Data

Webber, Marlene, 1947-
Food for thought

ISBN 0-88910-458-1

1. Food relief - Canada. 2. Public welfare - Canada.
3. Canada - Economic conditions - 1991-
4. Canada - Social conditions - 1971-
I. Title.

HV696.F6W42 1992     363.8'83     C92-095170-8

*For David, dear touchstone,*
*and for Nina, brave friend*

# Preface

IT'S PROBABLY JUST a personal quirk, but as projects wind down, I usually ask myself what images will stick. In this case, two linger. The first comes from Vancouver, where the food-bank is sandwiched between fastfood joints. In a quiet corner of one, I'd wolfed down a quiet lunch and was off to an interview next door. As I hurried away, from the corner of my eye I glimpsed a woman making a beeline for the table I'd just left.

Something made me turn and discreetly take stock. She was about thirty, presentable and unremarkable, except for the impression of invisibility she exuded. The woman sat in the seat I'd vacated, eyed my leftovers—soggy lettuce and an inch of cold coffee —picked up my cup, gulped the remains, then ate the scraps of salad with my fork. Without looking up, she stood and slipped out the back door.

The second memory comes from another city. I was standing around while volunteers handed out food hampers at a church depot. Boxes contained some canned goods, lots of stale bread and donuts. The volunteers were pensioners probably, and white. Most of the customers were young aboriginal men, many of them embarrassed and awkward. They'd come by foot that particular cold, grim day. A few carloads also came, about six people per car—if you could call their rusted-out old gasguzzlers cars. One of the volunteers whispered to me: "See that, they've got those big cars and they want free food.... What can you do? Can't teach an old dog new tricks."

COME THE FOOD drives, I, along with tens of thousands of Canadians, dutifully prepare a parcel of groceries. My small donations do not spring from faith in charity. They spring from fury at the existence of hunger in Canada, consumer heaven and bounty's heartland. And they spring from a feeling of utter hopelessness, given our irresponsible governments and lame social protections, of feeding the needy right now by means other than private handouts.

Delivering my parcel, packed with the typical poor-food items foodbanks request, makes me feel lousy. I feel rotten knowing I've been rooked into supporting something I oppose—charity as the answer to growing poverty. It burns me knowing that by helping to feed the hungry I capitulate to politicians who force the wrong people to pay for the economic crisis. It disturbs me no end knowing I help elected officials shirk their obligations to society.

In the short term, however, I cannot *not* contribute milkpowder, tinned meat and the like. If I refuse on principle, my principles cost my neighbour, and particularly her children, their dinner. I know full well if I stop giving groceries, governments would not start guaranteeing people a livelihood and dignity. Yet only un-willingly do I prop up a charity system that symbolizes so much wrong, gone worse.

Most of my acquaintances also abhor the charity "solution." They are sickened by the spectacle of fundraisers, where the *hoi polloi* dine on exotic foods so the hungry can eat humble pie. They cringe at news of benefit bingos, where the relatively poor gamble on their only hope, lady luck, so soup kitchens can afford to throw something in the pot for the absolutely poor. Yet, these crit-ics do just as I do—donate groceries, cash or labour to foodbanks.

This book comes out of a search for solutions to that dilemma. And it comes out of a conviction that we cannot accept private humanitarian aid in place of guaranteed human rights.

TO FIND OUT what foodbankers, the hungry and anti-poverty activists think about charity and solutions to pover-ty, in the spring of 1992 I asked some of them. I interviewed people in Halifax, in Saint John and Bathurst, New Brunswick, in

Montreal, Ottawa, Toronto, Burlington, London, Regina, Edmonton and Vancouver.

Several streams of thought and a few hot issues predominate throughout what insiders call the foodbank movement. I spoke with representatives of those crosscurrents in the Canadian Association of Food Banks (CAFB). To capture the movement's wider perspective, I studied materials published by the CAFB and by individual foodbanks.

Bear in mind, however, that foodbankers are far from a homogeneous group. Foodbanking depends on tens of thousands of volunteers, each with their own ideas. In *Food for Thought*, I try to distill the leading lines of commonality and difference that emerged from discussions and from background reading.

The book was researched in a breathless rush and written at breakneck speed. The scars of quick study include a reliance on secondary sources, primarily the *Globe and Mail* and other newspapers. Scars may include some misrendering of foodbankers' ideas. To limit that risk, I sent chapters that most mirror the movement to two insiders for review. This is not to suggest that anyone but I am responsible for any remaining errors.

Finally, something which should go without saying, but I want to reinforce it anyway: views not attributed to foodbankers in general, or to particular individuals, are my own.

# I

# The Rich Get Richer and the Poor Get Foodbanks

*Normalcy, where I went, is a state of siege. The abyss where men and women*
*with no homes or steady jobs find themselves is nothing less than a*
*slaughterhouse. It is very wrong indeed.*
—Alan Mettrick, *Last in Line*

O N THANKSGIVING DAY in one of the richest countries on earth, a tiny minority will gorge on any delicacies their hearts desire. A shrinking majority will splurge on a modest feast. A phalanx of about 3 million poor, still managing to scrape by without charity food, will buy whatever small treats they can afford. About another 2 million who've hit rockbottom will head for foodbanks and soup kitchens. Thousands of others, too shamed by handouts, will go hungry.

About 40 per cent of those scrounging for supper will be children. Another 20 per cent or so of adults who show up at public kitchens, or who cook up an ersatz banquet from donated, inferior ingredients, will have worked full or part-time that week. Others supping in church basements will have worked all their lives; as recently as last year some of these new poor could afford to buy fixings for a turkey dinner. The rest dining on free food won't have worked for a long time. They will be familiar with the ritual humiliations of holidays—those days on which their outcast status sinks in. Those days on which they most disappoint their kids.

An army of volunteers, many living one paycheque away from poverty themselves, will make it possible for those worse off to collect Canada's crudest form of aid. A few politicians will also pitch in, maybe contribute a frozen turkey as a photographer from the local daily captures the moment. Maybe wash a dish or two in the mission kitchen under the glare of television lights. When a CBC reporter hosting a lighthearted spot on hunger for the rolling-home crowd asks the dishwasher from the ruling political party what he thinks of all this misery, he'll praise the spirit of voluntarism. He'll hail the spartan dinner party as a community success story.

Even though the reporter won't pose pointed questions, the politician might offer a sound byte on the unavoidable pain of economic progress. He'll assure listeners that hunger, though regrettable, should be thought of as merely a necessary short-term cost of making the country "competitive" in the new "global marketplace." He'll invoke the mantra of the mighty: we must pay down the debt. He's bound to sneak in a cheer for "democracy" and the "free market." The outcome, he'll admit, isn't perfect. But, he'll add, let's not forget Canada is the best place in the world to live, according to the United Nations.

The politician certainly won't mention that the same UN report, full of rave reviews for this country, also showed the income gap here between rich and poor is nearly twice that of most other industrial countries. He won't cite government's own data proving our out-of-whack wealth distribution allows 20 per cent of families to hoard 43 per cent of all income. The bottom 20 per cent struggle along on 4 per cent.

Set against footage of downcast food lineups, his upbeat patter will omit the biblical canon he likely believes in: the poor will always be with us. That's the canon Thomas Malthus, an English political scientist who died in 1834, elaborated into a philosophy of poverty. Malthus pontificated that poverty is not only natural, but also necessary to check overpopulation. According to Malthusian math, the number of mouths to feed would always outstrip the food supply.

History, of course, has since disproved his thesis. Indeed, the problem of food scarcity was vanquished long ago. As Susan George shows in *Ill Fares the Land*, the world community produces bounty enough to offer everyone a decent diet, whether they live in opulent Canada or drought- and famine-stricken Somalia. The more important point, and the main one George makes in *How the Other Half Dies: The Real Reasons for World Hunger*, is that poverty is profitable. It is lucrative for, among others, the employer of cheap labour, the landlord who thrives on welfare cheques, and the price-fixer who controls food distribution. If poverty were not a moneymaker, in a world glutted with food, there would be no reason to starve people.

The media have made the spectre of mass starvation in under-developed nations, where the rich live and dine like kings, a commonplace sight. And beneath the pictures of hollow-eyed children with swollen bellies, too wasted to swat flies, the Malthusian axiom lurks: poverty equals fate. Moreover, misery's overwhelming scope, in Asia, Africa and Latin America, helps hucksters of the status quo convince us that nothing can be done about hunger, homelessness and ill health "over there."

But the chronic hunger affecting about 10 per cent of Canada's population is a much harder sell. So too is the general poverty claiming another 10 to 15 per cent. Poverty means lack of access to the income, goods, services and amenities generally understood as bottom standard within the country. Few Canadians, even those bamboozled by the shoddy idea of inevitable "Third World" suffering, believe poverty has to exist here. In our over-abundant and under-populated land, not many can be hoodwinked into thinking of hunger as natural.

However, many people have for now been sold on the idea of charity as the solution to poverty. It's an idea that owes itself to Malthusian logic. After all, if hunger is inevitable, then Mother Nature, not man the producer, bears responsibility for human agony. Human beings, then, may be able to mitigate misery through humanitarian aid, but we cannot banish want. Society may be able to cure some patients, but it is stuck with the disease of pauperism. The strength of Malthus's imprint varies with the times; today's massive network of about 2,000 food programs across Canada is high tribute to his ghost.

## Ottawa's Dirty Secret

TWO THOUSAND FREE-FOOD outlets. That number compares with 643 McDonald's franchises coast to coast and adds up to what Gerard Kennedy calls Ottawa's "dirty secret." Kennedy runs Toronto's Daily Bread, the country's largest foodbank. And here's what Ottawa is concealing: as the feds bow out of the social-security business, they surreptitiously create conditions forcing foodbanks into the frontlines. Then the mandarins go mum on the mounting hunger crisis. They clam up about the volunteer army slaving to satisfy basic needs, a job that legally and morally belongs to government.

Foodbankers don't slog away in the warehouses of the misery business because they picked charity as their choice solution from a range of options. Rather, they look upon their labour as practical necessity. They know many families cannot afford food. They know that, as a result, large numbers of children eat poorly, or erratically, and sometimes not at all. They know that as poverty runs amok, governments run away. Food-charity volunteers know all this because the bulk of them live a heartbeat away from need themselves. They cannot overlook hunger because, they fear, it might not overlook them. But, aside from collecting and handing out food, they don't see immediate alternatives for combatting the crisis.

They wish things were different. They wish, for instance, that food was something more than a commodity controlled by a handful of transnationals and regulated by profit margins. They wish sufficient food for everyone was a right in reality, not just a promise on paper. Indeed, many foodbankers uphold "food security" as an inalienable right. The Canadian Dietetic Association describes food security as "a condition in which all people at all times have access to safe, nutritionally adequate, and personally acceptable food in a manner that maintains human dignity." This definition captures the antithesis of what it means to depend on foodbanks.

The Canadian government has many times reaffirmed its commitment to everyone's right to life. And, as Susan George underscores in *Ill Fares the Land,* surely a right to live presupposes a guarantee of nourishment to sustain life. George reminds us that no other human entitlement has been so consistently enshrined in international laws as the right to food.

Brian Mulroney recently signed another promissory note, the "Convention on the Rights of the Child," ratified in 1989, that binds the state "... in case of need [to] provide material assistance and support programs, particularly with regard to nutrition, clothing and housing." Politicians love to strut on the world stage, issue high-sounding phrases and sign morally weighty documents like the children's convention and the UN's Declaration of Human Rights. Its Economic, Social and Cultural Rights Covenant, which Canada also signed, trumpets the "fundamental right of everyone to be free from hunger." The invisible subtext, obviously understood by world leaders, must read "everyone, that is, except the poor."

Government inaction, or ineffectual action on food security—or worse, hostile action stripping the people of essentials—infuriates foodbankers. Like the majority of her colleagues across the country, Jill van Dijk, who runs the Vancouver foodbank, believes most Canadians both want and expect government to guarantee life's material necessities. Ordinary people are in no mood to sacrifice social protections on the altar of a reduced deficit.

Van Dijk decided to press the issue of her province's failure to honour the freedom to food. Last year, her organization served notice on the ministry of social services, threatening to help welfare recipients sue the province through the Human Rights Commission. Van Dijk warned she'd take action if the welfare system continued to refer the needy to foodbanks, and continued to refuse them enough money to buy basics.

Shortly thereafter, the NDP came to power. The foodbank decided to back off, to give the new government a chance to tackle hunger. In particular, van Dijk hoped the bureaucracy would ease up on discretionary funds that, for a recipient, can make the difference between buying or begging for groceries. Many meetings with the ministry later, van Dijk says it's political business as usual. She finds the NDP more willing to talk, but no more committed than its predecessors to act on food security. "They want to study the problem, rather than solve it." Once again, the foodbank is gearing up to pursue a first human-rights case.

## Governments Choose Hunger

THROUGHOUT THE FOODBANK movement people believe hunger exists because those who control the country's purse-strings choose for it to exist. In picking whose needs and interests will prevail in tight-money times, those in control do not choose the chronic poor, the near-poor, the new poor and the about-to-become poor. Rather, they choose the rich, the richer and the richest.

Carolyn McNulty, who runs Romero House, a Saint John, New Brunswick, soup kitchen, feels that "government has never done what it should for the poor. But, if there were a [hunger] crisis of this proportion elsewhere in the world, they'd send emergency aid.... Here we get politicians coming around with a can of beans thinking they're doing a great thing."

Slow to honour fundamental rights and basic needs of vulnerable populations in the best of times, governments are quick to scrap social guarantees in the worst of times. It seems as if they cleave to only two kinds of ironclad promises: their pledges to hold onto power, and their vows to their corporate pals. After the New Democrats won power in Ontario, many in their cheering section, including poor people and their organizations, counted on the NDP to break the mould. But when the Party met in June this year for its annual convention in Hamilton, the Ontario Coalition Against Poverty (OCAP) was outside picketing. According to press reports, OCAP spokesperson John Clarke chided the Rae government for, among other faults, favouring corporations at the expense of workers, the unemployed and the poor.

When foodbankers and anti-poverty activists charge that governments "choose" hunger, they cite two primary proofs: social-spending cutbacks—more about that later—and antisocial spending. Indeed, almost everyone who contributed to *Food for Thought* condemned what they consider government spending atrocities. Contributors offered local, domestic and international examples, atrocious either for their flagrant waste or for their anti-people character.

From the onset of the 1980s, governments have been crying over their allegedly empty treasuries. Politicians in power at all levels claim they're doing the best they can, under near-bankrupt conditions, to offset the recession's impact. But foodbankers, like many other Canadians, see little evidence that government aims to blunt the blow on ordinary people.

Everyone points out that Ottawa and the provinces have found money to finance megaprojects, which generate private wealth, public debt and few permanent jobs. They've found boodle in the kitty to bail out big businesses. They've found cash to carry on globetrotting—now, in the spirit of restraint, in executive class, supposedly, instead of first! They've reached into their pork barrels to award lush severance packages to senior bureaucrats.

Recent press reports peg the federal unity tab at $100 million—but who knows how much higher the real cost may be? One wonders how many Canadians condoned the costly skirmishing over a Triple-E Senate as a more worthy ticket item than feeding our kids. How many thought it was more important to renovate the PM's residence than to put a roof over the heads of homeless people? How many would have awarded $4.4 billion to buy 50 techno-genius helicopters, most of them war machines, when Canada claims to be a peacekeeper? How many would have chosen to shell out $480,000 for the Queen's Concorde junket to visit us on Canada Day—yet another cash cow—when hunger haunts the land?

The Concorde, on a day when hundreds of thousands of our children didn't drink Kool-Aid, let alone milk, because their families couldn't afford it. This, the day before an estimated 20,000 Newfoundlanders were pinkslipped when Ottawa shut down the northern cod fishery, decimated after an orgy of government mismanagement and sellout of our seas. The fishermen got a $225-a-week "interim package" (raised to about $400 after a militant protest) while the Queen got the red carpet.

These travesties, picked at random from a cornucopia of contradictions between the interests of the government and the people, symbolize the values of those who manage the national treasury. Canadians can only guess at the overall cost of hidden spending antagonistic to the commonweal. Foodbankers tend to suspect an outrageous price tag for these travesties, both in terms of human tragedy and dollar value. Some put the Gulf War at the top of their list of recent moral/financial international atrocities. Governments "say they haven't got any money to feed the people," fumes Art Trovato, who volunteers at depot 7 in Vancouver, "but, by golly, they found a billion dollars real fast for the Persian Gulf," a war Trovato condemns.

Carol Goar, national affairs writer for the *Toronto Star*, described how craftily the federal government disguises where money for its priorities comes from. If Joe Public has the temerity to ask for a look at our collective bankbook, Revenue Canada will gladly send him a handy pie-chart. The sanitized graphic showing how each dollar is spent makes it look like every penny is accounted for.

But where on the chart, Goar asks, did money come from to pay for two typical miscellaneous items in April? For 22 corporate executives from companies like Northern Telecom and General Electric to jet along with Trade Minister Michael Wilson to China on a trade mission, at taxpayers' expense? Or, for 23 MPs and senators to schmooze with their Washington counterparts for five days at a Florida luxury resort?

In the overall scheme of squandered public money, these are nickel-and-dime offences. But a government begins to rankle when it gouges the public of its spare change only to indulge corporate welfare and the lavish lifestyles of those who betray the public trust. Indeed, many foodbankers are fed up with politicians who lack moral brakes, and who don't, as Art Trovato puts it, "give a damn about people."

But contributors to this book particularly take umbrage with the fortune various levels of government fritter away on studies about the poor, and about reforms to the welfare system. They reckon bureaucrats' shelves must heave under the weight of proof that the system, far from uplifting the poor, chains them to degradation for eternity.

Many people in foodbank and anti-poverty circles are convinced governments intend social research to placate activists and substitute for action. Some contributors suggest the penchant for studying a problem to death instead of cushioning people so they might enjoy decent lives is by now a hackneyed ploy. If the people get restive, calm them with an inquiry or a royal commission; use parliamentary road shows to create the phantom of a government listening to the populace and poised for progress.

Many foodbankers believe, and indeed, spending evidence supports, that coffers are much more flush than mandarins admit. Certainly, the staggering tax-grab by all three levels of government has ensured they won't go broke. The *Globe and Mail* reports that out of every new dollar individuals earned since 1990, the feds and the provinces taxed back 61.5 cents even before Canadians got their paycheques!

In spite of the tax throttle, there is no denying a relative scarcity of state funds. The issue, however, is not that less money exists. Rather, the issue is how officeholders spend public revenues, especially when people are hard-pressed. Do they covet cash for programs that guard as sacrosanct the rights of all residents to material and other necessities? Or, do they hijack the public purse for their pet projects, typically at odds with the public's priorities? Rhetorical questions? Yes. But they give pause to realize that poor and at-risk populations, now between a fifth and a quarter of the population, do not make it onto the state's shortlist. Rather, governments rank them last in line for financial leftovers.

This conclusion, obvious to frontline foodbankers, also echoes throughout the voluntary human-services sector. It emerges strongly, for example, in this year's update to the 1989 Regina Hunger Inquiry, which bases its conclusions on feedback from a variety of social agencies. The report contrasts governments' financial fawning over unpopular projects that benefit the rich with its evisceration of programs that benefit the poor.

Anti-poverty activists, foodbankers, and perhaps most Canadians believe the needy must, by right, have first claim on the shrunken public pot. But far from enjoying any claim at all, those most innocent in the creation of the deficit bear the brunt of belt-tightening.

## Pampering the Propertied

JOHN PASQUINI, WHO manages the foodbank Moisson Montreal, reminds us that we cannot argue with the logic of cutbacks. But where is the logic, he asks, in concentrating restraint in those sectors of the population that could not afford to share the burden even if it were equally distributed? Moreover, as Pasquini underlines, the feds are not spreading responsibility around.

They could do, if, for example, Ottawa chose to call in corporate markers. A good start would be the $8 billion in delinquent corporate taxes Revenue Minister Otto Jelinek acknowledged this year. Governments typically claim they can't chase deferred taxes because big foreign investors will run away and take all the jobs with them. Apologists for the tax-free riders neglect to mention what Mel Hurtig points out in *The Betrayal of Canada*: that foreign-controlled companies produce very few new jobs compared with domestically controlled companies. And while foreign corporations took about one-third of all profits between 1978 and 1985, they reduced the number of jobs. Nor do the apologists mention that Canada offers one of the lowest corporate-tax rates in the industrial world.

Or the feds could choose to disburse pressure for paying down the debt by tinkering with the income-tax system. They could attempt the audacious, which never seems to occur to Ottawa or to the provinces: make the poor pay nothing, certainly nothing more, and make high rollers pay high rates. Instead, they make low- and middle-revenue Canadians overpay to the point of impoverishment.

In *The Quick and the Dead*, Linda McQuaig explains how big business claims that due to the deficit, social programs are perks the country can no longer afford. She exposes how the monied have used tax overload and the debt bogey to help sell the message that social programs have to go. McQuaig asks: "With such a serious deficit situation, can we any longer afford such tremendous inequality in our society?... In the face of hardship, perhaps inequality is one of those luxuries we just have to give up—in the name of reducing the deficit."

Instead of giving up the luxury of inequality, our governments choose to intensify disparity by pampering the propertied at the expense of the disinherited. In the U.S., the trend towards coddling the rich while pillaging the poor has reached such a pitch that even heavy-hitters in both political parties break rank and carp in public.

Kevin Phillips, a former Republican strategist, topped bestseller lists in 1990 with *The Politics of Rich and Poor*, replete with a cover blurb by Richard Nixon. The book trounces Reaganite Republicans for spearheading a sleazier-than-usual decade of debt and speculation. The likes of Richard Nixon, hardly best pal to the poor, endorse books like Phillips' because their authors contend the economic system is just fine. What's the problem then? A crop of greedy individuals have momentarily subverted American fair play.

In *The Culture of Contentment*, a hot seller on both sides of the border, economist John Kenneth Galbraith, a lifetime Democrat, upholds the notion of a great democracy temporarily derailed. He argues that the rich and their executive committee—the government in power, plus the conciliators in opposition—have gotten too greedy for everyone else's good. So avaricious, they even oppose the poor's claim on crumbs. Between 1978 and 1987, policies partial to the contented minority propelled a 28 per cent increase in poverty, from 24.5 to 32 million.

A number of similarly popular books, as well as a barrage of magazine and newspaper articles, catalogue the intensifying polarization between private wealth and public squalor. The *Globe and Mail* recently reprinted a *New York Times* tidbit: between 1983 and 1989, the richest 1 per cent of U.S. households increased their share of private net worth from 31 to 37 per cent. By 1989, the net worth of the top 1 per cent, or 834,000 households, stood at $5.7 trillion. The bottom 90 per cent, or 84 million households, had $4.8 trillion.

A recent *Toronto Star* reprint from the *Philadelphia Inquirer* points out that if the pay-gap continues to accelerate at its current rate, early in the next century the top 4 per cent will earn as much as 60 per cent of the rest of American workers.

Canada is buddy-buddy with America in more ways than just the Mulroney/Bush mutual-admiration society. The paradox of poverty amid wealth also plagues this country. Here, according to the Ontario Coalition for Social Justice, the richest fifth owns 69 per cent of net wealth, the middle two-fifths 29 per cent, and the bottom two-fifths 2 per cent.

Indeed, most messages in the surfeit of new public-affairs writing from the U.S. resonate in the Canadian experience. Those writings catalogue how the state cossets the rich while shredding the already-inadequate social net that formerly cradled the poor. And the writings single out gross and growing tax inequities as the crucial cushion to those sitting atop the social-class divide—a message all too familiar to Canadians.

NOT ALL CANADIAN corporations and multinationals operating in the country have sailed smoothly through the recession. The economic freeze has iced some of the giants. The crisis has boxed some other champs of world capital into a tight corner. Canada's own Olympia and York owners, for example, even had to borrow $500 million from their private fortune in a bid to bail out their business and to mollify nervous creditors.

Clearly, economic chaos reigns supreme. It forces some tycoons to merge their businesses, and even swallows some empires whole. But, despite scorching losses for a number of conglomerates, the rich have a much better chance than anyone else of skating through the recession. Thanks to government policies both before and since the early 1980s, most are able at worst to retain their rank, or at best to skim more off the top. The tax system is one of the most lucrative mechanisms for their grabbiness.

Regardless of political stripe, postwar governments have raised income taxes while lowering corporate levies. These two sources of government revenue were roughly equal back in the early 1950s, as Mel Hurtig points out in *The Betrayal of Canada*. Since then, personal income tax has climbed to almost seven times that of corporate tax.

What's more, as the income tax rate climbs, the burden on the poor increases faster than that on the more affluent. The poorest fifth of Canadians paid 232 per cent more income tax in 1990 than in 1982, according to Toby Sanger of the NDP Research Group. In the same period, the top fifth paid only 82 per cent more.

Tory "tax reform" cut the rate for those earning over $70,000 from 34 to 29 per cent. No matter how much higher income soars —whether to $100 thousand or $100 million—only 29 per cent is taxed back. Rather, it's taxed back if its owner doesn't avail himself of a clever accountant and generous loopholes. Yet a poor person earning as little as $6,000, with no math whiz and no write-offs at her disposal, pays 17 per cent on each additional dollar earned.

Moreover, both Ottawa and the provinces have manoeuvred a host of measures that take much more from poor and middling earners than from the rich. GST is, of course, Exhibit A. Linda McQuaig notes that the tax was designed not only to hike revenues, but also to shift the burden of paying about $4 billion a year from corporations onto consumers. Between federal and provincial levies, consumers now pay about 15 per cent sales tax on almost everything they buy.

Not to be outdone by Ottawa in making the poor pay for the economic crisis, some provinces have upped their use of lotteries, offtrack betting and casinos. These ventures appeal most to lower-income people hungering for the big payoff to which they have no other access except gambling.

Meanwhile the rich enjoy many government-given escape routes from forking over much of their money. The first $100,000 of capital gains—money from the sale of business assets—is tax-free. Dividend income is taxed at a far lower rate than earned income. And let's not forget all the legalized petty larceny committed in the name of business expenses. *The Quick and the Dead* mentions that tax-law professor Neil Brooks has identified $8 billion worth of tax goodies in this category.

The 1987 "tax reform" reduced the corporate rate from 36 per cent to 28 per cent. But don't take this to mean that Ottawa bothers to collect the 28 per cent. Government's own data reveal that 93,400 corporations with $27 billion in profits paid no tax whatsoever in 1987. According to the Ontario Coalition for Social Justice, a group of giants, including Bramalea and Confederation Life, paid not a cent on over $100 million each of them earned in 1989 profits.

And how about the banks? Hurtig reports that they made $7.64 billion between 1980 and 1987, yet paid federal tolls of only 2.48 per cent. This despite the fact that the recession has set the banks rolling in unprecedented profit. They rake it in through outrageously high interest rates on credit cards, through laughably low borrowing rates for themselves, and through the tens of thousands of personal and small-business bankruptcies which allow them to clear out weak loans. Hence, the eight biggest banks posted 1991 profit increases ranging from 1.1 per cent for the Canadian Imperial Bank of Commerce to 23.8 per cent, or a cool $595 million, for the Bank of Montreal. In the first quarter of 1992, Canadian bank profits totalled $989.1 million.

The wealthy, in short, are swathed in perfectly legal tax-evasion opportunities. The tougher the taxman clamps down on everyone else, the more he slackens his grip on the financially blessed. By now it is virtually a shibboleth of Canadian governments that the rich have a right to be spared from paying significant taxes.

But tax breaks make up only one of many gifts governments use to sweeten the deal for big business. Monied interests monopolize other economic and social policies that have brought ruin to much of the rest of the population. The Free Trade Agreement, which Maude Barlow at the Council of Canadians calls the "corporate bill of rights," ranks with taxes in the Exhibit A department.

But taxes especially tie in to the discussion of poverty and hunger. That's because our relatively cash-strapped governments could choose to collect money from those who both own it and owe it, instead of from those who own little and who, by now, owe little or nothing. If the rich were made to pay their dues, the poor might finally collect their due.

### The Inner Circle Rules

POLITICIANS HAVE CERTAIN people in their back pockets, and that's all they cater to," says Vancouver foodbank volunteer, Art Trovato. Along with many others, he believes poverty and hunger swelling in the underbelly of plenty signal the absence of genuine democracy. Indeed, Canada's now deeply scarred socioeconomic record reminds us that the wishes of the majority do not prevail.

Trovato, who lived through the Great Depression, says that nowadays when he tries to get people to vote, they shrug and say "what for?" They tell him "whoever I vote for is not going to do a damn thing for me, number one. And number two, if I vote, I have no choice."

"Voting every few years, that's not democracy anyway," says Jill van Dijk, who heads the Vancouver foodbank.

Trovato, who has worked for the NDP, says an "inner circle" in political parties, including his own, picks candidates. He thinks ordinary people shy away from politics because they know who's in the driver's seat—and it's not themselves. He says the whole setup discourages participation. It robs people of hope they can make a difference or help bring about change.

Foodbankers like Trovato are not alone in their extreme disaffection from the political process. They are not alone in their frustration at finding no solutions in the halls of power to the explosion of poverty and hunger. Pick up any daily, or any news and public-affairs magazine. Read the letters to the editor. By tame Canadian standards of outrage, they ring with invective not only against Mulroney and his backroom boys, but against the way the political machine operates against the public good.

A typical letter, from Bert Hock of New Westminster, B.C., in *Maclean's*, reads: "While living in what is called a democracy, we actually reside in a semi-democratically elected dictatorship that has effectively hogtied the Canadian voter. We have been effectively and purposely kept incapable of influencing our governments at all levels.... Canadians are not being allowed to run the country."

If ordinary people were in charge, foodbankers believe Ottawa's "dirty secret" would soon be blown wide open and shut down. If the body politic controlled even shards of power, it would never allow the coming generation to grow up as children of charity.

# II
# From Emergency Stopgap to Welfare Prop

*It's very humiliating going to foodbanks, even if volunteers are nice people. You*
*never get over the feeling of humiliation, but out of need, you swallow your pride.*
—Violet Williams, Edmonton foodbank volunteer and user

ON THE DOWN side of town, neither hunger nor food charity are newcomers. Indeed, chronically poor families, especially those chained to welfare, can mark their year by handouts—Thanksgiving dinner in the church basement, the Christmas hamper, the Easter basket. And as many years ago as privileged kids started packing off to summer camp, underprivileged kids started trooping off to community halls for breakfast.

For decades, diligent charities like the Salvation Army have been quietly helping the destitute, supplementing barebones social benefits and low wages. Meanwhile, on the other side of town, the rest of us are bred to believe our "welfare state" takes good care of those who deserve it. Government largesse, we learn, even extends to unworthy layabouts who lose their ticket to a decent life by throwing it away themselves.

Until the 1980s, many baby-boomers, who hardly ever witnessed misery in the margins, may never have questioned the standard rendition of Canada the Good. Their parents, of course, lived through the 1930s when suffering broke loose from its neighbourhoods and streamed with fury into public view. But postwar prosperity, plus a patchwork of social benefits, eased the pressure on poverty's angry edge. As a result, from the mid-1940s to the early 1980s, want was almost invisible. Certainly poverty was hidden enough to comfort middle Canadians into doubting its grinding variety existed here.

Canada's self-image and image abroad featured a generous government which cocooned its few badly off citizens in an enviable social-security blanket. The picture of benevolence benefitted by comparing our rescue net with the shabbier version in the United States. Governments and the media never tired of reminding us how lucky we were relative to the Americans—which indeed we were. There, citizens only dream about medicare and welfare equal to ours.

But no one ever mentioned how miserly our social spending was relative to the rest of the industrial world. Nor did anyone mention how badly the States fared as welfare spenders. In fact, according to the Organization of Economic Cooperation and Development, among developed nations only the U.S. and Japan assign less of their Gross Domestic Product to social purposes than Canada allots.

Perhaps because the American standard has been the only gauge Canadians saw, many accepted the low benchmark of comparison. They concluded our assistance net was sturdy. Indeed, some believed the bricks and mortar of our social edifice could withstand a blizzard of economic changes. If things were to get worse, the helping system would surely respond by getting better.

Social activists, who knew better, tried to shake the public from its stupor. They struggled to get across how fragile and inadequate the rescue system really was. Their voices, however, were sidelined. Given their powerless position, the poor were easily ignored. Their allies, though less easy to dismiss, were written off as radicals. Politicians and the press were able to get away with treating poverty as a special interest, not as a mainstream issue. Until very recently, the subject of poverty ended up just where the poor ended up, and just where politicians wanted—in the periphery and under control.

Then, with the economic nosedive of the early 1980s, misery once again moved onto Main Street. Those already subsisting in penury sank deeper into its maw. People accustomed to living one pay packet away from poverty hit the skids. New paupers from the complacent middle bracket appeared on the scene almost overnight. Even before massive cutbacks warped the social-security screen, before unemployment insurance tightened up and welfare tamped down, the old charity circuit couldn't handle the new traffic. Overload particularly crippled the network in hardest-hit western cities.

Rumblings about hunger rising, even affecting people in leafy suburbs, did not outrage a public conditioned to ballot-box democracy followed by polite passivity. In the absence of an uproar, the political machine droned on as if nothing had changed. But, eventually, when it could no longer ignore the hunger crisis, government did respond—with cutbacks. And the deeper the desolation became, the deeper the state cut away social benefits.

Although the rumblings about hunger did not touch off curative government measures, they did spur the voluntary sector into action. Churches, already in the mission and soup-kitchen business, geared up to grow. Human-service workers discovered "surplus" food. In Edmonton, staff at inner-city social agencies, swamped by growing numbers of people needing basics, began to harp on the tragedy of waste, estimated at 20 per cent of food produced.

Then, in 1981, the first post-Depression foodbank opened in Edmonton. It billed itself as an emergency stopgap, soon to drift into oblivion with the return of good times. Instead, bad times worsened. Within a few years, foodbanks dotted the urban landscape of western Canada. A sprinkling of depots sprang up across the country. By mid-decade, about a hundred food charities had opened their doors. After that, the network grew like topsy.

By June 1991, the Canadian Association of Food Banks (CAFB) reported that foodbanks were operating or supplying about 1,800 food programs in 300 communities coast to coast. Countless other agencies, including major players like the Salvation Army, which include food services among their programs, were operating outside the CAFB orbit. Independents, not supplied by central clearinghouses, still cater to about 10 per cent of the hungry.

Foodbank use has risen astronomically. By March 1990, an estimated 1.85 million, not including repeat users, depended on free grocery and meal programs. That number represents a 53 per cent increase over a year earlier. The CAFB initially reckoned that in 1991 use would swell to 2 million, including 700,000 children. Although the official 1991 hunger-count wasn't tabulated by the summer of 1992, CAFB chairperson David Northcott revised the 1991 estimate to 2.4 million. There is every reason to speculate the actual number will prove to be 3 million before 1993.

Working from an emergency mentality, foodbanks started out in the early 1980s by supplementing, once or twice a month, basic groceries the family bought for itself. Emergencies quickly revealed themselves as everyday necessity. Soon foodbanks were handing out basic groceries. For some desperate families, depots become their main supermarket. Soup kitchens became their supplements.

NON-GOVERNMENTAL ORGANIZATIONS (NGOs) and churches propelled the new services, although trade unions contributed to their development in the West. NGOs, in particular, and faith-based groups continue to dominate the field. From the outset, governments, torn by conflicting imperatives, have played a shadowy and duplicitous role. On the one hand, they want to be seen as living up to their responsibilities under the Canada Assistance Plan, which promises everyone the necessities of life. On the other hand, as they recoil from their legislated and moral duties, governments need others to pinch hit for them.

From the start, the state resolved its dilemma by operating as foodbanking's silent partner. As Graham Riches explains in *Food Banks and the Welfare Crisis,* all three levels of government supported the rise of foodbanks as an opportunity to replace public assistance with private charity. Bureaucrats are not in backrooms venally plotting the emergence of foodbanks, as Gerard Kennedy at Toronto's Daily Bread points out. But, Kennedy adds, judging by their deeds, politicians favour privatization of public social services. They regard foodbanks as an "acceptable cost." At the same time, food charities annoy politicians because they catch the state in the act of sponsoring hunger.

Twitchy about foodbanks, politicians tend to keep a low profile on the subject. Nonetheless, they have been backstage from the first act, building the props. In some jurisdictions, they've provided startup funds, research support, low-rent or rent-free office and warehouse space. In other places, they've subsidized low-wage, short-term job placements.

Even Ontario's NDP which, to its credit and unlike other provincial governments, promised to eradicate foodbanks within its term, has backed down. Far from guaranteeing their demise, the NDP, over protests from foodbankers, last year set up a $1-million contingency fund for food charities. Foodbankers want the government to tackle poverty, not to throw high-publicity crumbs at hunger. The $1 million equalled $5 per individual using Toronto foodbanks the month the grant came down.

Politicians handle the heat they get over hunger by deflecting discussion. Alberta Premier Don Getty, for example, was quoted by the Calgary media for extolling foodbanks as part of Alberta's noble heritage of voluntarism. In an interview for this book, Nova Scotia's minister of community services, Marie Dechman, said, "In Nova Scotia, we're pretty community spirited.... I always believe that when things come from the community, they mean more."

Governments promote foodbanking by slashing social expenditures. In 1983 in Edmonton, for example, the province cut back shelter allowances to welfare recipients. Everyone knew this move would force recipients to fork over grocery money to landlords, in turn forcing the welfare poor into the foodbank. That's exactly what happened. As a result, two big shifts occurred. First, the number of member agencies joining the Edmonton foodbank shot up. Second, the foodbank had to go beyond supplying hampers to inner-city organizations and into supplying them for pockets of poverty all across the city.

The link between cutbacks and foodbanks is direct, swift and brutal. It doesn't take a cynic to wonder whether welfare ministers calculate the availability of free food into their restrained budgets for the poor. Or whether they count on charities to expand as social benefits contract. Doubtless, social-service mandarins quietly hoped the voluntary sector would take up the human slack created by a cutthroat economy and ruthless cutbacks. But the policymakers probably didn't dream foodbanks would not only accommodate government hopes, but far exceed them by building a massive charity industry within a decade.

WHAT THE PUBLIC thinks of as the main foodbank in their city is usually a central clearinghouse such as Moisson Montreal or the Edmonton Gleaners Association. The foodbank typically operates from a warehouse that ships groceries to scores of member agencies. Those agencies encompass every conceivable variety of human service, from old stalwarts like soup kitchens, to less traditional school lunches, to newcomers like AIDS hospices. Member agencies may share little more than a need for groceries to feed people who cannot afford to feed themselves.

Some foodbanks, in addition to supplying other food programs, run their own depots. The Vancouver foodbank, for instance, manages eight centres. One of them, in a sunny room with a friendly ambience evident when you walk in the door, serves only single parents and their kids. Another one, with 900 registered users, is notorious for long lineups that start at six in the morning, winter sleet or summer swelter—even though doors don't open until eleven. "It's like a cattle drive," complains Jill van Dijk, executive director of Vancouver's foodbank. Young mothers with their children and seniors queue up with drunken stumblebums.

Enormous differences, like the ones that divide these two Vancouver depots, also distinguish one foodbank from the next throughout the country. And between the extremes, you can find foodbanks and meal programs that, along with supper, serve up all hues of humiliation. Indeed, subtle shaming is endemic to charity. Open cruelty, although it exists, is exceptional.

Humiliation is one of many reasons why a new variety of foodbank controlled by consumers has come into being. User-driven depots vary as much as mainstream models. They cover the spectrum from nonprofit, neighbourhood food co-ops to collective food-buying clubs. Then there are originals like Community Unity in Burlington, a relatively affluent commuter city west of Toronto, where hidden poverty is on the march. At Unity, a group of people, who need food aid themselves, persuades local businesses and private donors to contribute groceries, clothes and household articles. Unity members take whatever they collect to their own homes, which serve as a chain of depots. Others who need free food call a central advertised number where a Unity member directs them to the closest home depot. In this scheme, both asking for and receiving food is a private affair, not a public one.

Many other meal programs struggle to keep users' dignity intact. They may charge for meals, if only a knockdown price. Multi Caf cafeteria in Montreal's densely populated Côte des Neiges district, and St. Francis' Table in Toronto's luckless Parkdale neighbourhood, operate on the pay-a-little principle. St. Francis' Table differs from your average restaurant in that cooks prepare dishes using donated ingredients, waiters and waitresses volunteer, and lunch and supper both cost $1.

Foodbanks and food programs, both those managed by users and by conventional charities, include an extraordinary mix of models. The best ones serve up only a soupçon of shame; the worst ones dish out degradation with dinner.

## An Army of Donors and Volunteers

NONE OF THESE free or near-free food programs, from most dignified to most demeaning, would be in business were it not for volunteers. Although Canadians didn't burst forth in rage over rising hunger, they broke out in empathy. Ordinary people dug deep into their hearts and their pockets, and they rolled up their sleeves. Almost overnight, an army of donors and volunteers marched eagerly into the war against hunger. Tens of thousands of unpaid workers have been in the trenches ever since—collecting, sorting and distributing an avalanche of donated food.

The CAFB estimates the value of food donations at $75 million a year. While it has not calculated the dollar value of free labour, cash donations and gifts in kind that keep its massive industry afloat, the price tag is way up there in the hundreds of millions. Daily Bread in Toronto needs $900,000 in operating expenses alone for 1993. Moisson Montreal spent $1 million to buy its own warehouse last year. Figures like these lead Edmonton foodbank user and volunteer Violet Williams to jeer society for its paternalism towards the poor. We entrust charities with money to feed the poor, but we do not put money into the hands of the poor so they can feed themselves.

In an epoch when sinking donations scuttle whole voluntary agencies, where does the money come from? It flows in from all kinds of sources: individuals, service clubs, church groups, small businesses and trade unions. Last year, in a first deal of its kind in Canada, the British Columbia Transportation Communications Union negotiated a $10,500 donation to foodbanks into its contract with Unitel Communications. Even foodbanks that don't actively chase dollars receive unsolicited cheques in the mail, usually for small amounts. The generosity stuns foodbankers, who remain flummoxed by the success of their enterprise.

And who contributes the approximately 50 million pounds of food a year it takes to keep the system running? Again, a broad spectrum of donors. The ratio of corporate to private donations varies widely across the country. In Montreal for instance, which depends heavily on donations from the food industry, private contributions accounted for less than 1 per cent of supplies collected in 1990. Vancouver, by comparison, relies mostly on donations from individuals. In 1990, private citizens pitched in 85 per cent of $1.5 million worth of food distributed by the Vancouver foodbank.

Nationally, the food industry accounts for 60 to 70 per cent of foodstuffs. Yet, according to business surveys by the Institute of Donations and Public Affairs, the commercial sector tends to be very stingy. In 1990, major corporations in Canada donated an estimated 0.60 per cent of pretax profits to charity. In such a tight-wad climate, why would the food industry, especially its fat cats, be so generous? Many reasons may underlie the gifts they give, but their main motivation, undoubtedly, is the money they save by giving.

Consumers pay for unsold food through pricing that covers "overhead" costs like waste and theft. But wholesalers and retailers lay out hard cash for trucking and dumping edible food they don't sell. By contrast, it costs them next to nothing when food-bank volunteers load and cart away garbage. That garbage consists mostly of staledated, mislabelled or cosmetically imperfect non-perishables, as well as production overruns.

Foodbankers point out that the food industry, canny about its giveaways, is loath to hand out items that affect profits. Wholesalers and retailers know, for instance, that poor people will spend their last penny on infant food. As a result, foodbanks frequently run short of essentials such as baby formula. But, because few people squander their last cent on nonessentials, charities are often overstocked with, for example, pickled peppers.

Depots can be over- or under-supplied with almost any item at any time. The food industry gives what it wants, when it wants. Individual donors give what they can of items foodbanks request, when they can. But because foodbanks cannot control the type of food they collect from industry, central larders, and hence individual hampers, rarely balance out nutritionally.

However, the chronic dietary deficits inevitable in a charity system unregulated by national standards proves to be a minor worry compared with the problem of donor fatigue. Food gifts, lifeline to the future of foodbanking, have been drying up. In some cases, foodbanks now have to hustle food corporations harder for spottier contributions. As the recession gets deeper, the industry tightens up on overproduction, yielding less waste for foodbanks to claim. Some smaller suppliers have gone bankrupt.

Food drives don't top their goals the way they used to. Gerard Kennedy says people feel they've given enough. Some simply can't afford to give any more. Other donors have themselves joined the breadlines. So, as hunger affects more and more people, donor burnout weakens the ability of foodbanks to respond. By 1990, close to 90 per cent of depots had resorted to rationing, according to the Canadian Association of Food Banks. Demand now significantly outstrips donations, and signals a crisis in the making.

THE U.S. PUBLIC, more than its Canadian counterpart, understands foodbanking as a savvy corporate activity. Here, supermarket chains collect good-corporate-citizen kudos for contributing to foodbanks. There, instead of public-relations spinoff, corporations collect big tax-breaks for donating inventory to charity. In fact, write-offs are so attractive that U.S. foodbanking has evolved into a highly bureaucratized corporate mission integral to the welfare system. Many Canadian foodbankers fear that the U.S. model will eventually take over here.

So far in Canada though, only the exceptional business seems to have finessed a tax deduction for food gifts to charity. Provincial politicians have only recently begun dickering over "Good Samaritan" legislation similar to that on the books in all U.S. states. These laws protect corporate donors and foodbanks from liability if contaminated food handed out in good faith causes illness.

Even though companies still risk liability in Canada, a remarkable cross-section of the food industry contributes to foodbanks: farmers, from dirt-poor independents to agri-businesses; farmers' unions; growers' associations; marketing boards; food-processing companies; wholesalers, and retailers, from mom-and-pop stores to industry giants. From the outset, industry has dished out the meat and potatoes of foodbanking. And foodbanks, not inclined to bite the hand that feeds them, return the favour by not scrutinizing food-industry practices.

CORPORATE CONTRIBUTIONS MAY be critical, but it's doubtful foodbanks could thrive without private donors. From their first appearance in the mid-1980s, food drives captured the popular imagination and made foodbanking Canada's charity of choice. Individual donations account for a whopping 30 to 40 per cent of central stocks. Fifty-six percent of people surveyed in a *Globe and Mail*/CBC News poll last year said they had contributed to a foodbank in the past year. One in four knew someone who needed a foodbank.

Who are these donors? Ask foodbankers that question, and from coast to coast you hear the same answer. People from all social classes toss tins into bins. But, everyone emphasizes, people closest to need give the most. The typical donor has either been hungry, whether recently or during the Depression, or now lives perilously close to poverty.

Food collection often amounts to strangers hurriedly dropping off a parcel to a volunteer at a firehall or other decentralized point. Hence, most foodbanks base their impressions about donors on appearance, neighbourhood, passing comments, even the cars they drive. Yet foodbankers offer remarkably uniform observations. Generally speaking, they say the people who can least afford generosity give most, while those who can afford the most give least.

Make no mistake. Aside from corporate Canada's care packages —money-savers for them—the noblesse, whether inside or outside government, are not feeling obliged to conquer hunger. But the beleaguered midsection of the populace is. The phenomenon of at-risk families shelling out makes sense when you consider the backdrop. As the recession guts middle Canada, workers know they could be the next victim of the economic shakeout—and next in the breadlines. Despite the much-ballyhooed "welfare state," they know unemployment insurance and welfare won't carry them far. Thus, they feel an immediate empathy with the new poor, and perhaps a newfound bond with all poor people. By raiding their own pantries today to help their newly disinherited neighbours, they buy bread for their own families for tomorrow.

The practice of the near-poor rescuing the poorer is nothing new, as journalist Alan Mettrick, author of *Last in Line*, discovered firsthand. Mettrick bummed around Canada for two years with transient victims of the early 1980s recession. He found that people who have known a "heaping of bad luck" help the down-and-out most. "It is fascinating how prevalent this is: the feeling, however subconscious, that by giving now you will get back later. It's a superstition, especially among those who have been down and know it might happen again. Ditch fantasy, they call it."

Many of those doing the scut work at foodbanks have lived in the economic gutter, or currently cling to its curb. Perhaps to an even greater extent than food donors, volunteers tend to be on intimate terms with hardship. They are welfare recipients, members of minority groups, disabled people, new immigrants, the unemployed, the working poor, low-income seniors and others on fixed incomes.

While they predominate, the already and almost-poor are not the only ones staffing this regrettable enterprise. People from every background do their bit. Desire to do something about hunger runs so high that volunteer coordinators work overtime slotting eager new helpers into incredibly complex schedules. Sometimes they turn would-be workers away. Whole classes of students, groups of freshfaced kids from the local Y, troops of boy scouts and girl guides wanting to pitch in, inundate food charities.

But there's a flipside to all this enthusiasm: volunteer burnout. Literally dozens of food programs have closed across the country because their benefactors simply got bushed from the backbreaking and heartbreaking work.

Foodbanks also tend to become what an observer writing in the *Toronto Star* once called "the human-service equivalent of the blue box." The comparison of foodbanks with the blue-box waste-recycling program sparked controversy. Yet foodbankers like Jill van Dijk, in Vancouver, themselves bemoan a hard fact of their existence: "A lot of people use [foodbanks as a place] to direct food that's not usable, or equipment that doesn't quite work, or people who don't fit in anywhere else."

The misfits include young offenders sentenced to community service in lieu of incarceration. They encompass others with all sorts of unusual traits and so-called special needs, individuals effectively locked out by the mainstream economy and society.

"Special needs" can mean anything from a quirky personality to profound disabilities. Foodbanks deserve praise for occasionally placing people our conformist society callously fails to accommodate.

Lots of volunteers brush up on social skills and enhance their resumé by working for a charity. But it's worth remembering that foodbanks can only welcome marginalized people as unpaid workers. A volunteer stint hardly represents a quantum leap from go-nowhere projects all too familiar to the poor. It hardly represents a rupture from sheltered workshops that exploit disabled workers.

VOLUNTARISM IS A muddled business marked by both pluses and minuses. On the plus side, volunteering does for many people what it did for Sandra Caulien. She's a former foodbank user, now employed by the Vancouver foodbank. "Volunteering made me feel I could give something back, not just take," says the young mother. For others, volunteering not only allows them to do something useful, it also helps shuck off two scourges of modern life: loneliness and isolation.

Few would argue with the value of volunteering, both for the individual and for the community. Many, however, question the use of volunteers as workhorses handing out basic necessities government is legislated to provide. Glen Pearson is not one of the questioners. Pearson, who runs the London, Ontario, foodbank and chairs the provincial association of foodbanks, lauds the use of free labour to deliver existing public programs. He believes Canada has been operating on a "justice model"—too much government help—for too long at the cost of neighbour helping neighbour. Now, thanks to foodbanks, he says that instead of "just paying taxes," "lethargic citizens" can get involved.

Graham Riches, author of *Food Banks and the Welfare Crisis*, also defends the importance of altruism. But, as he pointed out in a 1989 speech, altruism should serve as the lodestar of new social rights. It should cleave to its tradition of articulating and legitimating new rights. It should innovate services—AIDS hospices for example—

that respond to new needs. It should pave the way for governments to adopt progressive policies and programs. Riches believes the use of donated goods and labour to do the state's work perverts the value and vitality of voluntarism.

Yet tens of thousands of volunteers flock to foodbanks. It's easy to understand why. Making sure people have something to eat offers up an instant hands-on, feel-good cause to believe in. In part, the mass migration to food charities reflects the primacy of our need for food; everyone can relate to its importance. What's more, people realize that rites of preparing and breaking bread pull families together in an era when they are falling apart. Norma Jean Dubray-Byrd, who runs the Circle Project for native peoples in Regina, says we must not rob families of their few remaining roles by removing the rituals of dinner to the public arena.

The migration may also reflect the power of the press. Riches explains how the media have made foodbanks into the non-controversial darling of worthy causes. CBC and other radio stations even use their auspices and their premises for food drives. Gerard Kennedy complains the press love "powder-puff" stories and weepy anecdotes. But, as Riches points out, journalists hate to split open the hot potato that is the politics of hunger. They more often cool out contentious poverty issues. The media thereby help mislead the public into accepting foodbanks and voluntarism as appropriate responses to the atrocity of hunger.

However unwittingly, so too do foodbanks, volunteer staffers and private donors. And this is where the minuses of voluntarism kick in. Together, all forces propping up foodbanks fool us into settling for a superficial fix to a fundamental problem—the denial of basic rights. The idea of solving hunger by dropping off the odd bag of groceries to the CBC, or by sorting tins from time to time at a local depot, galls foodbanking's foes. Critics, such as the National Anti-Poverty Organization (NAPO), charge that food charities divert compassionate people clamouring for social progress into activities that support the status quo. Instead of hammering away at causes underlying poverty and inequality, the voluntary system papers over social sores.

## The New Poor and the Chronic Poor

WHO RISKS HUNGER in Canada? From the post-Depression era to the 1980s, the answer to that question was simple: people dependent on public assistance, and ne'er-do-wells dependent on the bottle. Over the past few years, however, entirely new populations of need, a solid majority of them employable, have bloated the foodlines. The rookies include middle-agers who've worked all their lives and who prize self-reliance with almost religious zeal. They've paid taxes and unemployment premiums without, in many cases, ever collecting welfare or insurance benefits.

Novices count among their ranks college and university grads chafing for their first crack at a career. Perhaps most disturbing, they encompass a growing number of proud, formerly self-sufficient seniors. Marjorie Bencz, who runs the Edmonton foodbank, says visits are so "dreadful" for older people that some prefer risking their health. Bencz, presumably hardened by long exposure to poverty's hurts, breaks down as she tells the story of a diabetic she served in the lineup. The woman had survived the Depression without assistance. She was determined to make it through again without help. But, after three days without food, she succumbed to charity. "We couldn't give her much because our hampers were pretty basic that week," Bencz laments. "To think this is our reward for someone who has contributed to society."

The new poor today rub shoulders with the hardcore poor: single mothers, their kids, disabled people and former psychiatric patients who've always had a raw deal. Poverty's complexion is changing so rapidly that its new face threatens to take over the profile. In this transition period, however, the traditional poor still need the lion's share of food charity.

A recent feature on foodbanks in *Canadian Social Trends* shows this to be the case. In 1990, 68 per cent of foodbank users relied on public assistance for the bulk of their income. They also needed two-thirds of 3.2 million grocery hampers handed out. That means the two predominant welfare groups, young families and

41

sole-support mothers and their kids, supposedly the deserving poor, suffer the highest rates of beggary in the country.

In 1990, less than 25 per cent of the population was under 18 years old. Although the innocents allegedly most coddled by government aid, children made up over 40 per cent of those eating charity food. One in every nine youngsters in Canada needed food relief 3.5 times in 1990. Young adults 18 to 24, like women, also suffer from more unemployment than other workers. When they do work, they are corralled into McJobs at McPay. Women earn about 67 cents on the male dollar; youths earn even less.

Yesteryear's conviction that hard work was a ticket to prosperity has become just another of today's mind games and con jobs. In 1990, 12 per cent of people straggling in breadlines did so after a week's work. In some cities, the employed poor today account for a fifth to a quarter of foodbank users. In the country's biggest, richest city, almost 20 per cent of foodbank households in 1990 listed employment as their major income source.

Breadwinners in these families may work one job, or juggle three or four. Foodbankers even see cases where several family members, each slaving at several jobs, cannot afford both to pay the rent and put food on the table. They are not the new poor, but the newly poorer, slogging harder, earning less. Their thinning pay packets are testaments to the new evangelism—making Canada competitive in the global market.

Their résumés often include a portfolio of course certificates. They've been "retrained" in unemployment insurance or welfare-sponsored programs. Recycled with outdated skills for nonexistent work, undertrained for high-tech openings, they job-hop from one crummy slot to the next. They hold what the now-defunct Economic Council of Canada calls "bad jobs"—meaning those characterized by low wages, shift work, part-time or seasonal work, few or no benefits, no security, no unions, no future.

Foodbankers take offence when people who work hard end up in soup kitchens. There's strong feeling out there in the frontlines that the indignity of food charity on top of disagreeable, underpaid jobs stretches the limit of civility. No one, food-bankers say, ought to do without what Canadians accept as the basic assets for dignity. The horrors of hunger, and the humiliations of begging for food amid wealth—these, they say, are travesties too great to heap on workers already dragooned into doing the dirty work.

L ATELY, THE NEW poor have joined the working and chronic poor in the lineups. Casualties of the recession, they come from an income bracket normally buttressed from the bitterness of hunger. But, in their hundreds of thousands, they've been bumped from jobs as businesses "downsize," go bankrupt, or, thanks to the Free Trade Agreement, go south to cheaper labour and laxer environmental laws.

The newly jobless, who may have lived paycheque to paycheque and racked up debt, quickly exhaust severance and savings trying to stay alive and to pay down the two-digit interest rate on their credit cards. For these un-preferred bank customers, a 6.5 per cent prime interest rate is irrelevant. They soon discover how tough it is and how long it takes to get unemployment insurance. Many first-time foodbank users report they're waiting for UI. Next time they show up, insurance has run out and they're waiting for government help. Finally, they're on pogey, dead broke and spiritually shattered by the triple shock of joblessness, welfare, and finding themselves charity cases.

The devastation newcomers initially feel is legend among food-bankers. Veteran food-charity worker Ed Bloos, who runs the Regina foodbank, has seen it all. His radar instantly picks out rookies. "They want to speak to me privately, to apologize and explain." Dianne Swinemar, who manages Halifax's foodbank, says it's grim handing out food to the new poor, especially previous donors. "You just know it's the most devastating experience they've ever had."

Daily Bread reports that nearly half the customers today at 200 Metro depots have lost their jobs within the past two years. Among those who sought hampers in February: 10,400 former factory workers, 5,900 laid-off office workers and 4,500 construction workers just off the girders. In all, almost 50,000 newcomers lost their jobs recently. Although numbers are less startling in some other cities, the trend is identical; people with stable employment histories are swamping the system.

Unlike many of their predecessors, daunted by weak schooling and functional illiteracy, the new poor tend to be better educated. In 1987, 13 per cent had completed high school, compared with 43 per cent in Toronto today. Even more worrisome, 25 per cent of the hungry in the city of the Dome have college or university training.

Lots of post-secondary students show up in the changing demographics of hunger as well. Last year, the University of Alberta opened the first campus foodbank. Others have followed, although students often prefer the relative anonymity of off-campus charities. According to Canadian University Press reports, tuition hikes, GST, loan and bursary cutbacks and a no-jobs economy are suspending or destroying many academic careers.

Foodbankers say that both well and poorly educated youth, especially males, drift across the country in search of work. Young transients, in a trend reminiscent of the Depression, are particularly evident in Alberta. In Edmonton and Calgary, migrants from the Atlantic provinces, Ontario and British Columbia account for 20 per cent of new welfare cases this year, the social services ministry reports. As well, unemployed Maritimers who went down the road are going back home in record numbers. Their return has spurred the growth of foodbanks in small communities where such services were unheard of several years ago.

When transients don't find work, they sleep rough and eat at public kitchens. Or they hole up in cheap rooms and hotels, often without a hotplate or a fridge. Boarders, both young and old, ask for food they can eat as is, no can opener or stove needed. Some wolf it down as fast as volunteers shell it out. "I see people grab food and eat it before they leave the building," says Eldon Anderson, chairman of the Regina foodbank. "Farmers come in so tensed up, we wonder if they'll walk out and commit suicide."

The degree of desperation of course varies from one individual to another. Ed Bloos says that "if every fiftieth guy I see has $2 in his wallet, I'm surprised." Bloos gets an inside peek at pocketbooks since his program obliges visitors to identify themselves with a health card. Every working day now, 4.5 families, most of them felled from the middle-income bracket, show up at Bloos' foodbank with an empty purse.

Chances they will become regular customers are outstanding. A minority of foodbank users need emergency help only. But the majority need it all the time. In Montreal, for example, frequent users rose by 67 per cent in 1991. The Bathurst, New Brunswick, foodbank estimates 80 per cent of its customers are regulars.

Chances are poor that frequent users in any city will be able to collect enough free food to hold the family over to its next bit of income. Most people who received groceries last year from Daily Bread agencies, for example, ran short despite the help.

The Edmonton Food Policy Council found frightening degrees of hunger in their city two years ago. The Council discovered 23 per cent of low-income families were accustomed to not eating for a day or more at a time. Lone-parent and two-parent families with children were hungriest. Parents gave what little food they had to their children, so their kids were "at risk" for hunger, or plain "hungry," instead of "very hungry." Twenty-two per cent of people the Council classified as "very hungry" didn't ask anyone for help; they went without.

Foodbankers meet the desperate who come to them, but they also know about the desperate who won't come to them—the hidden hungry. Many reasons compel people to suffer in silence. Pride and stigma induce invisibility, perhaps more so among the new poor than among the chronic poor accustomed to snoops and shame. But the welfare poor also worry about repercussions from the arbitrary, all-powerful system. What if a caseworker who's gunning for a recipient hears that her children are hanging around foodbanks? Many poor families fear the bureaucracy will snatch their kids; some prefer hunger to the consequences of being dubbed incompetent parents. No wonder many Canadians choose starvation over charity.

### Private Wing of Public Welfare

A MULTIMILLION-DOLLAR, nonprofit, volunteer-run system to collect and distribute free food to over 2 million people now operates coast to coast. It's not surprising, therefore, when critics conclude that foodbanks have evolved into the private wing of public welfare. Even some friends of foodbanking admit that foodbanks, contrary to their intentions, have becomes fixtures in a failed social venture.

Graham Riches says that en route to arriving at permanence, foodbanks helped governments hide the breakdown in public welfare. Foodbanks, he says, symbolize the breakdown and help perpetuate its legitimacy. By helping the state shirk its work, food charity becomes "part of the problem of pervasive hunger and malnutrition in Canadian society."

Pierre Legault, ex-manager of Moisson Montreal, sees no way out for foodbanks at this point. Yet he sees their work as handing out "wasted food to those society treats as wasted people." Karen Shaver, a former foodbanker who organized Toronto's Second Harvest, agrees. A recent *Canadian Forum* article on "Food Banks and the Politics of Hunger" says Shaver now believes foodbanking is "a secondary welfare system which provides second-rate food to people who have been obliged to become second-class citizens." NAPO has called foodbanks "accomplices" to government in its abdication of statutory social duties.

Governments at all levels depend on foodbanks as much as the hungry who use them. Ottawa and the provinces accept private charity as a substitute for public justice. If they did not, they would buffer the needy with basics. If they opposed the charity solution, politicians would not polish their image by using food drives as photo opportunities. They would not behave like hypocrites, hyping their party's efforts to solve hunger while casting cans into a container. If they did not condone foodbanks, governments would prohibit caseworkers from referring a steady stream

46

of customers. It is one sure measure of political support when welfare workers serve as a key conduit for newcomers.

In effect, the two systems, public and private, work in tandem. Most food programs don't hand out hampers in the week or two following welfare "payday." Charities kick in the other two weeks of the month after the cheque runs out. Painkillers, not cures, the two systems now accomplish poorly what one used to manage less badly—postponing hunger another few days, but solving nothing.

# III
# Cutthroat Economy and Ruthless Cutbacks

*Childcare is now considered a last priority.... I had the privilege to be [its] killer.*
—Health Minister Benoit Bouchard, February 29, 1992

B RIAN MULRONEY AND his Tories have distinguished themselves as the most unpopular leader and governing party in Canada's history, according to the pollsters. Political fortunes, of course, have been known to flipflop. The Conservatives could even recapture power. It partly depends on how their constitutional gambit plays out, and how much the economy heats up before the next election. What if a swift and startling recovery—an unlikely turn of events, admittedly—were to put Canada back to work? Given an economic about-face, mightn't Mulroney become man of the hour? But if the economy continues to stagnate, or dives from recession into depression, the electorate will certainly turf the Tories.

The point here is that we are led to believe that all things afoul in the land spring from the current regime in Ottawa. If things were good, or if they were to get better, we would also be expected to believe that Mulroney magically improved them. Thanks to the great-man theory of history on which we are weaned, our fate supposedly devolves to one omnipotent leader. That individual, usually but not always a man, may indeed be great, or for that matter, godawful.

The current fashion of Mulroney-bashing, though warranted, makes too much of the man and too little of the economic and historical conditions in which he operates. Instead of dissecting those conditions and exploring how to change them, ardent anti-Mulroneyites heap all the blame on one politician and on one political party. And, as logic goes, if these two indeed are the root of all evil, then we need only replace them with another leader and another party embodying good.

Which leader? Which party? Jean Chrétien and the Liberals, the party which long ago sold Canada out to the highest bidders? Audrey McLaughlin and the New Democrats, the party which in power distinguishes itself only marginally from the Liberals? How about the new gang on the old, moribund political block, Preston Manning and the Reformers? Would musical chairs among these players result in making the rich pay for the economic crisis? This is a question worth pondering as we lambaste the current batch of rogues in power.

Leadership, of course, is critical, but it does not function in a vacuum. Mulroney and his crew had a lot of help remodelling the country into a caricature of what Canadians want. They had help from a world recession. They had help from an economic system with a built-in boom–bust cycle. They had help from the legacies of previous governments, which had many years earlier begun dismantling postwar social and economic gains. They had help from foreign owners to whom Canada was already enslaved when Mulroney came to power.

Amid the anti-Mulroney mania, let's not forget where Canada stood at the zenith of Trudeaumania. Offshore owners, mostly American, held the country's resources and industries in their grip. So thoroughly had the long-reigning Liberals sold out Canada that we were subject to more foreign domination than any other industrial nation on earth.

True, except for the 1930s and the early 1980s, this downturn breaks previous records. And true, Ottawa's policies have clearly exacerbated rather than modulated the effects of the underlying crisis. Without doubt, Mulroney's posse has ridden roughshod over the country, designing more than a typical Canadian government's share of disasters for the people. The crisis, however, is not, as many suggest, "made in Canada." Rather, it is made unnecessarily worse by a government that disdains its people.

Take the GST for example. Before the tax, seniors were noticeable for their absence in foodbank lineups. But, since the tax, they've been showing up in large numbers. The GST shoved some people on fixed incomes over the line between coping and collapsing. The Tories understood that any new regressive levy would drive vulnerable seniors to ruin; yet they chose to collect revenues in a way that would make it happen.

Tory policies provide a rich mine of similar examples proving how they've chosen to aggravate, rather than to soften, the effects of the economic upheaval. But worsening a situation, which by its nature gives rise to crises, is not the same as creating it. Saying Mulroney caused the shambles is a bit like saying a man beat his wife because he was drunk. A surface explanation, it overlooks the roots of violence. It leads us to want to fix the man, or to urge the woman to replace him with a better model. It does not lead us to expunge the roots of violence so that society stops producing beaters.

By the same token, shovelling blame on one individual or one political party leads us to replace them with another leader and party. It distracts us from the search for systemic causes. And this, in turn, sidelines us from the quest for systemic solutions.

Besides, we delude ourselves if we think Canada was bound for economic and social justice before the inglorious gang conquered the Hill. Amid all the anti-Mulroney rhetoric, though wholly justified, recall that pre-Tory Canada was disfigured by 7 per cent official unemployment and 14 per cent official poverty. Before Mulroney, in the glory days when federal coffers overflowed, more than a million children subsisted under the poverty line. Long before he assumed power, the country contended with a dollar democracy in which money moves freely to wherever return is highest, never where human need is greatest.

WHAT'S BEST FOR big business is what's best for the bottom line. And government in practice, though not in democratic theory, is above all about protecting bottom lines in good times and in bad. In good times, it's about ensuring that transnationals, homegrown and foreign, expand their advantage. In bad times, it's about, at the very least, safeguarding them as much as possible from sinking into the red.

These biases held office long before Mulroney did. They didn't always wreak as much havoc as they do today because earlier economic conditions favoured more liberal social protections. But in the economic zero hour, overkill in government efforts to help corporations stay out of the red produces worse-than-usual consequences for ordinary people.

Aside from all the other destabilizing forces at work, the technological revolution alone has intensified chaos in the economy. Companies "downsize" and "rationalize." Technology allows them not only to save costs by replacing workers with computers, but also to boost production. Statscan reported that although employment fell by 0.5 per cent in the first quarter this year, productivity grew by 0.4 per cent. Trimmed labour costs, hand in hand with higher outputs, excite the apostles of "restructuring," who nonchalantly separate the marvel of technology from the misery it creates. Masters of industry and state seem to regard displaced workers as expendable human dross, worthy of little more than a let-them-eat-cake attitude.

But cheaper labour costs depress workers. They're out of wages at a time when social expenditures are bad for the bottom line. There have been times when social expenditures were good for profits. In the 1960s for instance, while the economy was expanding, governments sank a fortune into health, education and welfare. The investment produced a healthy, viable workforce. At that juncture, a massive social outlay suited conglomerates. No one hinted to Canadians, however, that any bond existed between social benefits and big-business interests. No one warned us that when social programs outgrew their value for the corporate ledger, people would lose their benefits.

Rather, the Liberals sold us a public-relations fable on their motives for social policies. As a result, many baby-boomers grew up believing benefits were gifts from a Robin Hood government. Like the vast public, the government believed in greater fairness, so it took from the rich and gave to the poor.

Despite this fantasy embedded in the Canadian psyche, in fact no such redistribution occurred. In *The Canadian Family in Crisis*, sociologist John F. Conway shows that income policies never shifted money from top to bottom. Rather, they hitched low-income families onto state subsidies for their puny share of the pie. Yet, this truth conveniently disappears under heady claims about Canada's Cadillac of social-security schemes.

The notion that the country's social bulwark buffers people in bad times is another swindle about our safeguards. And it is one coming undone with a vengeance right now. Myth has it that if the economy sours, or if individuals fall down for any of a variety of reasons, the net catches them. In fact, the rescue provisions work best in more prosperous times. Despite what we've been led to believe, government does not bank social premiums so the needy can collect higher benefits when their fortunes bottom out.

The system is light years from such sensitivity. In fact, it shuts down in direct proportion to social needs notching up. Indeed, as the volume of the economy shrinks, so too do social expenditures. They shrink because social spending, formerly a boon to business, becomes a millstone around its neck. That's patently obvious now, as industry sloughs off workers the way they dump dated equipment in the slag heap. And Robin Hood? Nowhere in sight.

What's more, during economic crises, governments go into overdrive to buoy big business. This is the route to recovery, they claim. Partly, governments prop up commerce by siphoning every available cent into the corporate sector through bailouts, giveaways and tax breaks. Part of the padding for the rich comes from social padding stripped from the poor, and from middle-income earners. It comes from savaging health, education and social-security budgets.

The looting leads to an increasingly polarized society character-ized by paltry benefits for the poor, inferior services for the lower echelons of the middle class. Only the upper-middle class and the truly rich retain the edge over everyone else. Only they can afford to purchase university education or the services of a medical spe-cialist. Does this script sound familiar?

### Bye-Bye Universality, Hello U.S.A.

THE DOCTRINE OF universality, responsible for efficient monthly mailings of family allowances since 1945, dies this December. Only big business and their Ottawa bagmen will enjoy the funeral. In *The Quick and the Dead*, Linda McQuaig ar-gues that fundamental changes to our social safeguards go to the heart of the "business agenda":

> Social programs represent an egalitarian, community-oriented ap-proach to society that has no place in the new global marketplace. If Canada is to become truly lean and world-competitive, it will have to shed the notion of itself as a society with high uniform standards guar-anteeing equality in some of the most crucial areas of life—health care, education, social security.

McQuaig shows convincingly who is behind the demolition of benefits: the Business Council on National Issues (BCNI), the Canadian Chamber of Commerce and the Canadian Manufactur-ers' Association. In *Parcel of Rogues*, Maude Barlow describes the BCNI as the "blue-chip lobby group for corporate Canada." It rep-resents the 150 fattest corporations, banks, insurance companies, oil and gas firms and foreign multinationals such as Xerox, IBM, and IT&T.

Why waste public money, BCNI and its colleagues ask, on peo-ple who don't need it? Why send baby bonuses to K. C. Irving's family or old-age pensions to Conrad Black's? Why not simply target the needy? Because, as Maude Barlow says, targeting trans-forms benefits from a right to a charity. Such a shift, however, lit-tle disturbs those who never have to shop at Goodwill. Hence, BCNI et al. blithely lobbied for the demise of the only income

54

schemes that do not stigmatize the poor, and that do benefit the vast majority.

Universal social programs enjoy immense popularity. Indeed, it's probably fair to say Canadians regard old-age security and baby-bonus cheques as birthrights. That must be why Mulroney promised he'd guard the "sacred trust." That popularity certainly explains why he hesitated to murder universality in one blow. Instead, Mulroney chose death on the installment plan. The Tories hit first in 1987 with their attempt to claw back, from higher earners, both pension and baby benefits. Clawbacks set the stage for this year's final assault. By the same token, the 1992 axing clears the path for a coming wave of attacks that could culminate in the end of medicare.

McQuaig cites warnings from health economist Dr. Michael Rachlis. He says that when Ottawa stops transferring health dollars to the provinces in 2002, regions will be left cash-strapped and unable to maintain national health-care standards. Inevitable user fees could usher in a two-tier system: private medical clinics for the rich, and an underfunded, rundown public system akin to Britain's for the rest.

McQuaig also chronicles the rising chorus of business voices hectoring for "quality over accessibility" in our universities. If they have their way—and government cuts thus far suggest they will—our education system will gradually resemble the élitist American model. McQuaig believes our system now works as a "great leveller." While mounting evidence shows that this isn't the case, we have every reason to fear that the system's capacity to equalize opportunity will worsen drastically.

BUSINESS AND GOVERNMENT collaborated to kill universality in two vital social programs. Undermining national standards augurs ominously for the frayed remains of the social-security net—and for health and education, also on the hit list. Here's what *Unequal Futures: The Legacies of Child Poverty in Canada*, a recent report from the Child Poverty Action Group, says about universality:

Universality ensures that benefits and services are made available to everybody on equal terms rather than being confined to the poor. Parents, regardless of their level of income, can proudly accept their Family Allowance cheque because they receive it in recognition of the extra costs involved in child raising and not because they are living in poverty or are labelled "needy." Experience has shown that services and benefits directed at the poor alone soon become poor programs as middle-income people see themselves no longer having a stake in defending and improving them.

With the end of programs that, to a small extent, homogenize social classes, the poor are destined to further alienation from the mainstream. And any measure that distances the poor favours a U.S.-style social fabric. Such a fabric policymakers are now busily spinning for Canada.

### Tory Tenets: Anti-Women, Anti-Child, Anti-Family

BETWEEN 1984 AND 1988, the Tories whittled over $100 million from statutory social programs, according to the National Council of Welfare. Yet that's a pittance compared with the hatcheting they've done since. In the frontlines of hunger, disgust runs high on social-policy reversals. And, of all the programs governments have crippled or scuttled, no losses rankle foodbankers more than the ones affecting women and children.

In a telltale preamble to what this year's federal budget had in store—the death of daycare and baby bonuses—Health Minister Benoit Bouchard told the House of Commons last December: "I believe that money does not fix any problem that children have in Canada." In keeping with this nugget, and despite runaway child poverty, the Tories held the line on child-related spending. Well, not exactly. They did manage to milk an extra $135 million from the budget over the next five years for Ottawa's one existing childcare subsidy—tax deductions that favour rich families with kids in daycare.

University professors Anthony N. Doob and Neil Brooks did a little math for the *Toronto Star*. They calculated that a single mom with $25,000 taxable income, who spends $5,000 on childcare, will receive a subsidy around $1,340. A two-parent family earning $150,000 will receive $2,450, almost twice the poor mother's benefit. Because it reduces taxable income, the childcare expense deduction offers tax savings that increase with income.

While the Tories conferred this tax break on rich parents, they upped their frontal attack on poor parents. Bouchard set the stage for the mass-execution budget by creating a false dichotomy between childcare and child poverty. He claimed his government could only afford to do something about one of these issues. Furthermore, he claimed that Canadians care more about kids at risk of poverty than about kids without daycare. This phony gulf between inseparable problems pitted groups desperate for affordable childcare against each other: employed women with average earnings, against unemployed mothers.

Bouchard's ploy was tailor-made to distract the public from the substance of cuts and losses. But few were fooled. Under the cover of duplicitous and confusing chatter about a "new integrated child tax benefit," Ottawa killed daycare and family allowances. It replaced the lot with a flimsy new program.

The net result of the re-jigging? Zero dollars for the unemployed poor, and up to a maximum of $500 a year for the working poor, if they earn $10,000. Even the insulting $500 vanishes if a family manages to earn $26,000. The *Toronto Star* quoted working-poor, single-mother Josephine Grey: "All that government bull about millions of poor families getting higher benefits just isn't true."

Indeed, Finance Minister Don Mazankowski lauded in his budget banter a "substantially enriched" child-benefits package. But in fact it puts only pennies in the pockets of the poor. The changes will, however, enrich Ottawa's coffers. *Maclean's* reported that the feds will scalp $750 million through its supposed new deal for kids. That's nice candy coating on top of the $1.2 billion Ottawa already bilked from child benefits over the past eight years, according to social policy researcher Richard Shillington.

Reaction to the rearranged child benefit, along with Ottawa's $500-million "Brighter Futures" program to combat child abuse and poverty, was swift and caustic. Shillington told the *Globe and*

*Mail* that inflation will quickly erode the new benefit because it is not fully indexed. "It's putting child benefits on an escalator that's going down," he said. Jean Swanson at End Legislated Poverty in Vancouver says the sales job on the package was "absolutely slimy." "It's a 20-watt light bulb," Gerard Kennedy told the *Toronto Star*. Daily Bread's director added that the new program doesn't come close to replacing the $1 billion the feds robbed from Ontario's poor by cutting back Canada Assistance Plan transfers.

Barbara Kilbride, executive director of the Canadian Day Care Advocacy Association, voiced a common complaint: "You can't talk about child poverty without talking about childcare." Susan Sullivan, from the Canadian Council on Children and Youth, worried the money might go to a "glitzy poster campaign." Indeed, everyone suspected an advertising bonanza, a fear which has since come to fruition in "Children Matter," a series of tepid TV spots. A government that could have chosen to give families cash to feed hungry children, chose instead to bankroll its own image as caring.

### Dismantling the Sacred Trust

IN 1990 OTTAWA capped the growth on its social-transfer payments to British Columbia, Alberta and Ontario at 5 per cent a year. These jurisdictions, Ottawa claimed, were wealthy enough to carry the financial burden of swelling welfare rolls. Before this drastic measure, under provisions of the Canada Assistance Plan (CAP), the feds underwrote 50 per cent of welfare costs, while the provinces and municipalities set the rates and paid the rest.

Ottawa's move provided three premiers with a perfect whipping boy on which to blame deteriorating conditions. The provinces hid their unwillingness to make provision of basic necessities the number-one priority under a barrage of blasts against Ottawa. The feds, in turn, badmouthed the provinces. The war of words was a typical political setup: both sides accused the other while neither got down to dealing with the business at the heart of the dispute—hunger and homelessness. Meanwhile, within the three provinces, tensions flared between municipal and provincial governments. They wrangled over financing for a variety of local welfare-related services, which were being stretched beyond capacity.

While politicians jockeyed to score points, poor and at-risk populations sank deeper into despair. Repercussions were so keenly felt by foodbanks that at its annual meeting this year, the Canadian Association of Food Banks (CAFB) demanded Ottawa remove the ceiling on CAP and refrain from imposing it elsewhere.

By the time most poverty newcomers found their way into welfare offices in both capped and other provinces, payments had been curtailed. Rates weren't necessarily cut, though for certain categories of recipients, particularly single "employables" in some provinces, they were. More typically, eligible applicants were forced to choose between very low or no assistance and workfare.

Quebec led the pack. Bill 37, introduced in 1989, reduced benefits for about 80,000 recipients. The bill created conditions for herding the poorest people into the worst-paying jobs. John Kinloch, spokesperson for CAFB and director of the Multi Caf community cafeteria in Montreal, says the consequences of Bill 37 were devastating. People who refused workfare became much poorer. Those who accepted also became poorer because their combined wages and supplement fell short of their previous welfare income. The bill drove people, who had been scraping by, into foodbanks.

Elsewhere in the country, rates which hadn't risen in years and were absurdly out of sync with the cost of living, still didn't rise. In addition, the system netted big savings by axing non-standard or supplementary benefits.

These extras include a range of special-request items granted or denied at the discretion of individual caseworkers or offices. The list varies but covers things like first- and last-month rent deposits, moving allowances, food vouchers, some prescription medicines, transit passes, non-emergency dental care, basic furnishings, and assistive devices for disabled people. Not exactly luxury items. Rent deposits, for example, make the difference between housing and homelessness.

Carolyn McNulty at Romero House in Saint John, New Brunswick, scoffs at these cutbacks. "I guess you're not allowed to get ulcers if you're on welfare, or have allergies, or need special diets." McNulty claims that even diabetics are denied extra food allowances.

Many welfare workers oppose the cruelties they've been forced to impose. Severe cutbacks and vaulting caseloads make a mockery of their mandate. The credo of casework: assist people financially over the short-term, and help them cobble together a better-than-welfare life for the long term. Hyperbole even in good times, these promises ring even more hollow in bad times. How can a worker handling 424 cases, the current Toronto average, help all applicants process the requisite forms, let alone get a life? A worker told the *Toronto Star* she might be able to do her job with a caseload of 150.

She and several of her colleagues described the big-city welfare office of the 1990s. Bulletproof glass and locked doors separate applicants from workers. Surveillance cameras and uniformed guards patrol edgy crowds in packed waiting rooms. Guards stand ready in case a frustrated applicant being interviewed in a secure cubicle loses his grip. "What [applicants] expect from us and what we're able to do for them are at opposite ends of the pole," the caseworker said.

## Shredding Unemployment Insurance

BEFORE 1990, UNEMPLOYMENT insurance offered vital protection during gaps in employment. For all its flaws, UI not only paid better than welfare, it also cost less in lost dignity. But, two years ago, in keeping with its gospel of unfettered cutbacks, the federal government enacted Bill C-21. The bill overhauled UI into a job-retraining and shadow welfare scheme. By tightening eligibility and shortening benefit periods, the reconstituted version of UI helped flatten wages and create a workforce desperate enough to accept lower pay. It primed the unemployed for sinking pay just as the 1990 recession started to cook.

❖

In the same blow, Ottawa shifted the entire burden of UI premiums onto workers and employers. Workers would pay through wage losses and employers would pay by passing their costs along to consumers. This cozy rearrangement pleased the business lobby which had been urging its boys in Ottawa to ransack the too-generous program. The Mulroney hatchetmen reckoned they'd save $1.3 billion and disqualify about 30,000 applicants. The critics estimated C-21 would knock about 130,000 formerly eligible workers off the UI payroll.

Politicians, particularly then-Employment Minister Barbara McDougall, tried to sell their wanton calamity as an improvement. To do this, they created a brouhaha over new UI-sponsored training, claiming that learning opportunities would catapult workers into new careers. In light of what has since happened—Ottawa treated training as just another bargaining chip in the constitutional discord—the training ruse seems particularly cruel.

Labour, anti-poverty and women's groups organized a "Save UI Day" this summer. These groups worry that in the devolution of federal powers to the provinces, nothing is precious. They fear protections will scatter and diminish. They fear national standards for training and rates will vanish. They fear the advent of a U.S. clone where states compete to attract investors by undercutting premiums. In addition, they know business favours emasculating UI. Corporate Canada prefers the decentralized American model because it pays fewer workers smaller amounts for shorter periods. Maude Barlow at the Council of Canadians reminds us that 80 per cent of unemployed workers collect UI in Canada, compared with 25 per cent of American workers.

Perhaps the biggest clue to nefarious plans for UI can be gleaned from the number of politicians who this summer publicly denied the program is up for grabs. Recall that vociferous denials preceded all major attacks to date on social programs.

## Closing the Door on Housing

OUTPRICED HOUSING IS the second leading factor, after low incomes, forcing families into foodbanks. The poor are trapped between the pincers of ridiculously low wages or welfare, and ridiculously high housing costs. Foodbanks across the country report that landlords gobble up well over half, typically 60 to 70 per cent, of the meagre pie on which poor families subsist. And to pay the landlord, their number-one fixed cost, people scrimp on the grocer. Among the home-owning new poor who frequent foodbanks, making the mortgage means missing meals.

In the insuperable challenge of finding affordable housing, many poor families live from a suitcase. Fran McDougall at the Matsqui-Abbotsford foodbank in British Columbia says that an area grade school lost an entire class over one academic year; every child in the room moved at least once to another school district. Foodbankers easily spot the children of this nomadic existence—they're the rudderless ones.

Many foodbank families lack all sense of security. Volunteers report that a disproportionate number of their customers butt up against bigotry in the private housing market. Many landlords reject certain prospective tenants on sight, particularly members of racial minorities and welfare mothers. These prejudices, combined with social-housing cutbacks, force families to live on the cusp of homelessness.

While percentages vary from city to city, most people who need free food live in private, not in public housing. Given that rent is such a culprit in the hunger crisis, it makes sense that poor people in rent-geared-to-income housing would have less need of food handouts. That's all the more reason, one would think, for Ottawa to pay special attention to housing disadvantaged Canadians.

Apparently not. During their killing spree this year, the feds finished off state-assisted cooperative housing. From this myopic move, Ottawa will save $25 million over the next five years. Most of the 164,000 Canadians on waiting lists will likely lose their last scintilla of hope for secure, high-standard housing. By moth-balling the co-op program, Ottawa shortcircuited access to the only top-calibre living conditions most poor people dare dream of. Because low- and moderate-income families, plus a scattering of higher-income households, all have a stake in them, co-ops avoid the ghetto taint of housing projects.

The government tried to wheedle out of this nasty blow by blaming the pullout on their concern that too few poor people end up in co-ops. Finance Minister Dan Mazankowski made a touching speech about how Ottawa wanted to ensure that scarce housing dollars benefit the most needy. His suggestion, however, that Ottawa was shifting support from co-op to social housing, was, to use national affairs commentator Carol Goar's words from the *Toronto Star*, "simply fraudulent." The budget not only dashed co-ops, it also cut down a federal promise to spend $97 million on other forms of assisted housing to $70 million. The slash will add up to an estimated loss of 12,000 affordable units over the next two years.

Goar described the co-op action as "dismantling a vital bridge from poverty to self-sufficiency," and "cutting off the country's supply of a modern and adaptable form of housing." A raft of national organizations—anti-poverty, labour, housing and charita-ble—besieged Ottawa to recant. The pleas were to no avail.

As to Ottawa's claim that co-ops veer from their intended pur-pose and house people who can afford alternatives—there is a kernel of truth. In Toronto, for example, only 18 to 20 per cent of the poorest people manage to get into government-subsidized co-ops. According to *Eye* weekly, more than 60 per cent of residents earn between $35,000 to $50,000—hardly millionaires, but sub-stantially healthier than the hardcore poor. Skewed distribution of units, however, doesn't impugn the nature of co-ops. Rather, it gives rise to questions about government management of its programs.

Besides, Ottawa's own data, cited by Goar, on the profile of co-op residents countrywide suggest that the needy do predomi-nate. Two-thirds of co-op households earn under $30,000 a year.

Single mothers, most of them working, head almost a third of the families. Some groups who endure the toughest time finding affordable housing—natives, recent immigrants, disabled individuals and older women—are overrepresented in co-ops.

The attack on co-ops inflamed foodbankers. They know only too well that many of their customers, even given today's rising vacancy rates and declining rents, will be the last accepted and first evicted. They know the private rental market is not motivated by human rights and social needs but by the lure of maximum profit.

That motive does not mesh well with the economic means of soup-kitchen customers. It does not complement the special requirements of some foodbank populations. For example, landlords don't want to risk disturbances and property damage from violent men tracking down the women trying to flee them. Yet battered women and their children rank among the most desperate for both safe "bridge" housing and permanent places of their own. Without assisted housing, where can they live?

Many landlords close the door on anyone they suspect might suffer from psychiatric disorders. Under the progressive rubric of "de-institutionalization," most of Canada's mental hospitals have been padlocked. Politicians promised decent homes and community services would replace the drugged-out warehouses of neglect. Instead, they abandoned a huge pool of bewildered people to the streets. Disoriented, often homeless or huddled in decrepit, unregulated rooms, they live at the caprice of boardinghouse keepers. Without assisted housing, where can they live?

Former psychiatric patients and battered women comprise only two of many groups with compelling need of subsidized housing. A growing mass of just plain-poor folks are equally desperate. But instead of first assisting those in the worst straits put a roof overhead and food on the table, Ottawa made it easier for people with RRSPs to buy a bungalow. The new break reduces minimum down-payments to 5 per cent, and lets first-time buyers use RRSPs. Although a welcome move, note the pattern it follows: perks for professionals balanced by policies that persecute the poor.

Residents and foreigners alike cherish an idea of Canada's health, education and especially our social programs as humane. And while the spin doctors, for their own purposes, have exaggerated Canada's generosity, we have enjoyed better services and protections than American citizens.

But, all of that is under attack now. Ottawa's slashers had a major go this year at the underpinnings of social security. Indeed, the death of universality marks a turning point in a sustained campaign to dismember public services and safeguards. It probably signals Ottawa's plans to finish the job it has started.

The social net is on the ropes. Postsecondary education as we know it could become a closed book. Medicare may be hanging on by a suture thread. There are no maybes, however, about the fact that Canada is open for business. Ottawa has shown a nothing-is-sacred eagerness to trim vital social spending its business buddies condemn as flab. Government has handed the most powerful free-marketeers *carte blanche* to redraft the social blueprint. In her 1991 preface to an updated edition of *Parcel of Rogues*, originally published in 1990, Maude Barlow makes a sad and telling comment: "Clearly, the concern I expressed in this book for the future of our social programs underestimated the speed and ferocity with which government is dismantling them."

That speed and ferocity have resulted in a booming business for foodbanks, which cannot keep apace, let alone ahead of demand. Foodbankers are running out of patience with the make-the-poor-pay policy. It's not surprising, therefore, that many who contributed to this book question the kind of top officeholders we've managed to end up with—individuals glib about the sufferings of ordinary people. Foodbankers want to know where the democratic ideal of accountability is hiding. Where is morality? Where are principles? Where are leaders who represent the people? Where is the "Canadian way," the ideal we treasure about ourselves?

THE STREAMLINED MERGER between two old partners, corporate boardrooms and political backrooms, has yielded the predictable results: a sweeter deal for the rich, hell for the poor, and life in a vise grip for most everyone else. Deprivation and privilege continue to span out to their extremes of absolute privation and absolute power. Governments have sealed the poor off from some amenities they customarily collected. The economy and harmful policies have bludgeoned many of the moderately comfortable into slots vacated by the poor. And pressure continues to squeeze down on those clinging to slightly higher ground.

The now-defunct Economic Council of Canada warned this summer that one in three Canadians will experience poverty during their working lives. Although an exact head count is elusive, poverty very likely touches the lives of one in four Canadians already. Officially, a 14 per cent poverty rate has blighted the country since the mid-1970s, even during peak-employment periods. But Statscan figures, though alarming, camouflage poverty's epidemic sweep.

In *The Canadian Family in Crisis*, John F. Conway mentions three caveats worth remembering about government data. They underestimate the extent of poverty. Low-income cutoffs are arbitrary and ignore almost an equal number of near-poor Canadians. Many of the officially poor suffer from extreme poverty.

Just as government figures, though alarming, mask the real extent of the poverty crisis, so too do they mystify the actual rate of joblessness. When Statscan announced that unemployment hit 11.6 per cent in June, an eight-year peak, the bad news was far worse than admitted. That's because Statscan reports exclude "discouraged workers" who weren't working the week prior to the survey, and who didn't look for a job the month prior. Reports also ignore masses of underemployed part-timers as well as full-timers in the swollen ranks of the working poor. Although these groups have jobs, however tenuous, they cannot make a living. Full-time, minimum wages, in 1990, at best paid under $10,000, or 40 per cent of government poverty lines.

To make matters worse, the value of minimum wages has eroded steadily. Since the 1970s, it has fallen by 20 to 45 per cent. Consequently, it took 65 to 80 hours of work to support a family in

1991, according to the National Action Committee. The Edmonton Food Bank estimates that a single parent with two children must work 98 hours a week for the family to touch the line. Moreover, rising to official poverty levels, because they are so low, carries with it only the hope of subsistence, nothing more.

Between March 1982 and March 1983 the welfare caseload countrywide soared by 23 per cent, and has since remained higher than ever before. About 2.28 million people collected public assistance in 1991. Newcomers tend to stay on the dole longer than they did before the 1980s. Unemployment insurance, now effectively a parallel welfare system, also reports that workers apply more often and that their job stints between claims are shorter than in pre-recession years.

Conway confirms that poverty tends to be chronic, not fleeting, especially for single mothers and their children. While some people experience only brushes with poverty, or occasional bouts of it, for many others indigence persists from cradle to grave. Indeed, it often stretches its sticky fingers beyond the grave to thwart the lives of the next generation.

THE OFFICIAL PICTURE of poverty disguises just how far some folks have fallen. Many welfare rookies, and thousands of tyros tramping the free-food track, may never before have seen close up how the other fifth lives. But today, conditions force some former residents of the fragile middle-income cocoon to take refuge in soup kitchens.

Statscan data on income disparities maps the evictions from middle-income grace. Average family income rose by 22 per cent between 1971 and 1979. However, between 1980 and 1989, average after-tax income barely budged. The years 1980 to 1984 in particular evidenced a slumping proportion of mid-income families as their share of income sagged from 56.2 to 55.4 per cent.

*Unequal Futures* from the Child Poverty Action Group records the same pattern. Between 1965 and 1988, the middle fifth of the population lost ground. In 1965, it owned 18 per cent of total income; in 1988, 16.9 per cent. The report underlines how significant

1 and 2 per-cent shifts can be. For instance, in 1988, the top fifth gained 1.8 per cent of total income, or about $3.8 billion.

Profound flux in the economy and curtailed social spending undermine suburban stability. Most readers probably realize that cutbacks garotte the already poor. Fewer may know that these social-security subtractions also spell destitution for mid-income earners. That's because, as Conway explains, their proportion of income made up from social benefits almost doubled, from 5 per cent in the 1950s to 9 per cent by the 1980s. Hence, cutbacks, though more subtle in their effects on the suburbs than on the inner-city, nonetheless help choke off the relatively comfortable from their former good fortune.

Perhaps the most important question to raise about the fate of middle-income earners is: what has happened to them since 1989, especially after the recession heated up once again in April 1990? While the statistical verdict is still out, the anecdotal verdict from foodbanks is in: the stratum of the famous "middle class," to which the majority of Canadians supposedly belong, is fast on its way down.

### At Least 2 Million Poor Kids

NEW YORK, THE United Nations, September, 1990. Brian Mulroney, representing the country with the second highest child-poverty rate in the industrial world, enjoys a great honour: he co-hosts the World Summit for Children. His government follows up with a pledge to obliterate child poverty in Canada by the year 2000. Then, in the two post-Summit years, the feds launch one salvo after another against conditions that foster childhood well-being.

Foodbanks, among others, record the startling results: huge numbers of children hurtle into the jaws of poverty. In its 1992 annual report, the Canadian Human Rights Commission issues its assessment: Canada's international reputation as a human-rights hypocrite is growing. This country abrogates its international and domestic obligations to children. It shows "plain disregard for one of the most vulnerable sectors of our society."

*The Canadian Family in Crisis* charts that disregard. In 1971, 1.7 million, or one in four children, were officially poor. By 1980, although child poverty still thrived, in absolute numbers it had been halved. But, in the 1980s, more extreme child poverty made a comeback. By 1986, one in six was officially poor, half of that number "very poor." About another million were "near poor."

Statistics are, as Canadian poet Milton Acorn once wrote, "cold things." What a colder chill then to put the data down and conjure up a city the size of Montreal populated with hungry and near-hungry children. This inside the same country the UN hails as the best spot on the globe.

World-class Canada pits the needs of two of its most fragile groups—children and seniors—against each other. Government policies transferred to seniors part of what they took away from children over the last decade. In 1990, officially 15 per cent of seniors had low incomes, compared with 28 per cent in 1980. By contrast, 17 per cent of children were poor in 1990, up from 15 per cent in 1980. Rather than eradicating poverty, or even significantly reducing it, government just juggled the poor. For the past decade that juggling act has consistently sent children and young families crashing through the social floor.

Throughout the 1980s, even during the mid-decade economic recovery, child poverty persisted at about 15 per cent. This figure discounts tens of thousands of native kids subsisting in inhumane conditions. It ignores perhaps another million youngsters teetering on the brink. Then, from 1989 to 1991, the situation worsened. Statscan reports that child poverty shot up to 17.4 per cent, or one in six kids. The National Anti-Poverty Organization (NAPO) pegs the real number closer to one in five. There is every reason to assume the toll continues to climb.

MOST POOR KIDS live with two parents. However, the best prescription for child poverty is female single-parenthood. *Unemployment: Its Impact on Body and Soul* by the Canadian Mental Health Association (CMHA) details the drastic deterioration in women's situation. In 1977, 47 per cent of single mothers with young children were poor. By 1987, 56 per cent were (compared with 18 per cent of single fathers, according to NAPO). The leap occurred in spite of two major changes supposedly heralding heightened prosperity for families: government boosted some child benefits, and women poured into the workforce.

Most went to work because they had to. Conway concludes that married mothers burst onto the job market because serious declines in real family income hit youngest families hardest. As *Unequal Futures* highlights, by 1987, only families with two full-time earners risked poverty less than they did in 1973. And while females pried their way into some male strongholds, employers herded the majority of women straight into the "lace ghetto."

As of 1988, Conway points out, 73 per cent of all working women found themselves in clerical, sales and service jobs, or in teaching and health services. He reminds us of their "double segregation": relegated not only to the worst-paid sectors, but also to the bottom of those sectors. To this day, women remain ghettoized in low-paid service drudgery. In 1990, the Canadian Advisory Council on the Status of Women announced that women who began in the workforce's lowest echelon in 1980 were still trapped there a decade later. This year, the Council reported that women's underemployment or involuntary part-time work has risen by 41 per cent since 1990.

The recession, regressive taxes and social-spending reversals have deepened female dread. The triple whammy clobbered sole-support mothers. Whether working or welfare dependent, over 60 per cent were officially poor by the mid-1980s. Statscan reports that these worst-off families plunged 6.4 per cent in average after-tax income between 1989 and 1990. Two-parent families with one breadwinner dropped a steep 5.5 per cent, while those with two earners fell by 1 per cent.

The setback among poor, single mothers is particularly noteworthy given U.S. developments. Canada prides itself on being more socially progressive than its neighbour. Yet, the government axe cuts deepest here, like there, in the most desperate homes.

There, politicians are on a rampage against the poorest of the poor, particularly black, sole-support welfare mothers. To justify massive cutbacks, leading lights of both parties blame poor women for society's ills. Politicians target the women Ronald Reagan referred to as "welfare queens." George Bush likens their dependence to narcotic addiction, while Dan Quayle dismisses their plight as "fundamentally a poverty of values."

The impoverished values of absent fathers in arrears on support payments command less scrutiny. Yet in Canada and the U.S. the failure to fork over financial support compounds the dire straits single mothers face. *Unequal Futures* reports that parents in this country default on between half and three-quarters of support orders. While enforcement has improved recently in some provinces, many men go missing and others are too poor to pay.

To risk living at the bottom of Canadian society, however, a woman does not need an irresponsible or impoverished male partner. "Unattached" women endure crippling rates of economic marginalization. The CMHA report says that 75 per cent of never-married single parents live mired in economic misery. In its 1992 annual update of women's status, the National Action Committee alerted women to a bleak future: about 75 per cent of females live out the last quarter of their lives in poverty.

NOTIONS OF DESERVING and undeserving poor, left-over from last century's British Poor Laws, are deeply imbedded in Canada's welfare practices. These practices punish the poor for their predicament. Ironically, even the supposedly deserving poor, such as disabled people and single mothers, have never earned state subsidies near-equal to government poverty lines.

As the National Council of Welfare details in *Welfare Incomes*, the deserving poor receive about 60 per cent of what Ottawa deems the low-income floor. The state reckons that the undeserving poor, particularly young "employables," are even less worthy. In 1990, single people were entitled to between 24 and 60 per cent of poverty lines, for a national average under 43 per cent. In New

Brunswick, for example, that meant a jobless young man could receive $250 a month.

Yet starvation rates, even during a no-jobs recession, are little wonder when we recall that the social net weaves itself around an underlying assumption: losers author their own misfortune. If only the dullards would get up off their duffs and do an honest day's work, they too could be winners—an unrelenting theme in anti-welfare histrionics. This quote from the *Toronto Star* attributed to Ottawa businessman Ron Laporte is typical: "If the carrot was cut and people were a little hungrier, they would go out and put in a day's work." Laporte is described as "a self-made entrepreneur who dropped out of school and built up a successful construction business."

"If the carrot was cut" assumes what the notion of undeserving poor has always promoted: that public assistance undermines the work ethic. The logic goes likes this: welfare recipients need the spur of poverty. Freezing rates at rock bottom will prod the sloths into the workforce.

# IV
# Losers in a Fair Game

*A society that has given up the quest for social justice has lost its way. A country that has abandoned its weakest members is no longer a vibrant democracy. When the Donald Trumps speak of freedom, it is of freedom from democracy.*
—Maude Barlow, *Parcel of Rogues*

IN JOBLESS TIMES like these it's hard to believe that old myths about the poor still stick. You'd think firsthand experience with economic fragility would startle its victims into re-examining the causes of chronic bad luck. You'd think economic upheaval would jolt its witnesses, waiting in the workforce for their turn at joblessness, to look anew at poverty. You'd think we would all question our mental reflexes about the poor. You'd think, in short, that in times like these the ideology of the lazy bum would come undone.

Indeed, myths about the poor and the causes of poverty are finally unravelling, but slowly. Strands of blame-the-victim thinking still cling, even among foodbankers. In fact, some of them are obsessed about "abuse" of their system and are constantly on the lookout for freeloaders. A number who contributed to this book themselves raised the issue or cheating without prodding.

But probe a little, and surprisingly, even the most vituperative volunteer describes a particular profile of the so-called abuser. Most people who finagle every possible scrap of free food from the system suffer from some combination of three problems: an extremely dysfunctional family background, several generations of welfare, and psychiatric disorders. In other words, people who fleece foodbanks tend to be deeply troubled, even out of control.

When asked what percentage of customers break the rules, the detectives estimate 3 to 5 per cent. That's just below the 3-to-7-per-cent range in which officials peg welfare fraud.

And yet, despite the system's longstanding evidence, augmented by volunteers' own experience confirming a low incidence of abuse, many foodbankers fixate on fraud. They can't wait to tell their favourite story of some guy lollygagging on the public purse and filching food from foodbanks. Why? Some contributors, embarrassed by the overemphasis on cheating, speculate that the fixation derives from the myth of the welfare bum. Apparently, the myth is so entrenched, it even blinds some people to evidence they see with their own eyes.

Joan Turbitt at Community Unity, in Burlington, Ontario, confirms that "abusers" she meets fit the demoralized profile. Turbitt says "straightforward crooks" also burgle the food system just as they take advantage of any system they can crack. She contends, however, that because of overblown press, their charity scams loom larger in public consciousness than their small numbers warrant.

Turbitt wonders whether some people who harp on abuse have a hidden agenda. "Maybe they look for volunteer work in situations where they can have a lot of control." But even she recognizes how insidiously the mythology works. "I occasionally find myself wondering why a certain person needs free groceries. I have to stop and ask myself 'Why am I even thinking about this?'"

When questioned about abuse, Dianne Swinemar at the Halifax foodbank answers: "That depends on what you mean by abuse.... If a time ever came when I had to ask someone for food and they said, 'You can't have any from [this foodbank] because you were here two weeks ago,' I'm not sure that I wouldn't try to go somewhere else to get groceries for my girls."

Swinemar reminds us that abuse usually means one thing: rather than sticking with a single outlet and taking home one, maybe two hampers a month, people make the rounds. They canvass a variety of depots in hopes of collecting one food basket a week. A tiny fraction of these collectors may, as rumour has it, re-sell rather than consume the groceries. But, as Lise Corbeil of the National Anti-Poverty Organization (NAPO) points out: "People don't go begging because it's fun. They certainly don't go begging for three-day-old bread to sell for profit!"

Foodbankers call making the rounds "double-dipping," and it is verboten in practice if not in policy. So verboten that in a bid to halt the habit, some agencies within the same district trade information about people who use their services. Some employ their own means test—less sophisticated than a welfare quiz, but the same idea.

Apparently some foodbanks go to great lengths to ferret out very few cheaters. How come? Because, they say, fraud stories are magnets for the media. Bad press can devastate their fund and food drives. In addition, demand overload can empty their chronically understocked shelves. Turbitt thinks these explanations justify outmoded attitudes. She challenges her counterparts to use their position to shred the myths rather than to snare the cheaters. Don't misunderstand. She's not advocating a free ride for crooks. But she does want the spotlight shifted onto myths about the poor.

In the midst of this touchy subject, it's worth remembering most foodbankers assume only desperate people turn to them. They take for granted that most so-called cheaters cheat because they need to. Foodbankers recognize that a once- or twice-monthly hamper doesn't assuage hunger.

PUBLIC OFFICIALS ROUTINELY reinforce the idea of the poor as con artists enjoying a cushy life on the dole. A recent example: earlier this year some Toronto city councillors alleged widespread welfare fraud. That led Metro to review 780 calls to its "snitch line." The *Toronto Star* reported the results. Of the alleged offenders, 509 weren't receiving welfare. Sixty-three were disabled or single mothers. Only 15 cases were worthy of inspection. It turned out that officials were already investigating four. Three of the remaining 11 warranted study. In other words, from 780 calls, the fraud squad netted leads to three possible cheaters!

Even though officials have long known the facts of fraud, some of them continue to peddle lies. Joan Turbitt claims that "when they need to justify cutbacks, bureaucrats and politicians are quick to scream, 'We need more fraud investigators.'" Their entrenched victim-blaming attitude echoes throughout society. And while some foodbankers themselves subscribe to the ethos, more of them complain about their encounters with what they consider ignorance.

Carolyn McNulty at Romero House in Saint John, New Brunswick, offers this example: "Just because we're in a spanking new building ... I've had higher-ups in the Church say to me, 'Wouldn't the poor be more comfortable in an older building?'" She rebukes people who expect the luckless to look downtrodden and to settle for shabby conditions. "Some people will donate spare change to a derelict, but they'll turn on their heels when a panhandler looks cleancut."

Dianne Swinemar knows what McNulty means. She tells a story about meeting with "upstanding churchwomen from a very affluent Halifax neighbourhood." They were choosing a charity to receive $300 they'd collected one Christmas. "The previous year, they'd sponsored a family, but when so-and-so delivered the food and gifts, she doubted whether the family needed them. The little girls were dressed really nice, stockings were hung, and decorations were everywhere.... What are people supposed to do? Give away ornaments they collect over 20 years, give away clothes they've accumulated?... People who need assistance don't dress in rags or live in huts!"

Not only are the deserving poor expected to look stricken, but they are also expected to act grateful. The same contributors to this book who emphasized abuse, often complained about ingratitude, or enthused about grateful "good clients." They also tended to play up drinking, gambling and bad budgeting.

Let's not romanticize here. Lots of poor people drink, drug or gamble away whatever money the landlord doesn't scalp. Some smoke like chimneys. Their kids gorge on junk food and they squander their precious few dollars on designer togs. So do scads of other people in other income brackets. Where is it written, food-bankers ask, that the least privileged must be the most saintly?

Swinemar questions why some volunteers "get all upset" when a foodbank user takes a cab home. If customers don't have other transportation, if they've got groceries in hand and kids in tow, what else can they do?

Many contributors pointed out how the powerful employ special standards for judging the powerless. It is commonplace, for example, to hear that poor people incompetently manage money. How often do we hear that same charge about the non-poor? Why does budgeting, contributors ask, figure so prominently in analyzing the problems of people who have no cash to count?

THERE IS LITTLE doubt that intergenerational welfare breeds demoralization in the bone. Long-term contact with the system tends to reduce people to what Fran McDougall at the Matsqui-Abbotsford foodbank in British Columbia calls "life in the comfort zone." By that, McDougall means a bottom-of-the-barrel mental rut from which its inhabitants neither see nor dare dream of an exit. They accept the welfare "comfort zone" as their natural place in society.

In theory, public assistance supports people at a culturally set standard, through temporary doldrums, whatever their cause. Simultaneously, it helps them harness external and internal resources to forge ahead and reclaim self-sufficiency. In practice, prolonged exposure to the system often crushes self-esteem and hopes for a better life. It diminishes many recipients until they succumb to a psychological cellar and abdicate responsibility for their lives.

Many studies have catalogued how the welfare system irreversibly hitches some people to handouts for life. Some, who've known nothing but poverty and government cheques since they were born, become welfare junkies and spend their whole lives up against the system. Manipulating foodbanks fits in with their normal survival mode. As Rob Henderson, former head of the Halifax foodbank, once said: "They have begun to accept that they should be using foodbanks, that they aren't entitled to anything more." More astounding than the fact that a few people cheat, however, is the fact that so many who have been brutalized by poverty don't.

### Tallying Poverty's Toll

RAPID-GROWTH CANCERS, hunger and want feed on the flesh of moral fibre. Evidence of the ethical slide ratchets up as the recession hunkers down. "There are more and more pressures on responsible behaviour and the gap is growing between espoused values and actual practices," David Nitkin, president of EthicScan Canada, told a meeting of the Canadian Centre for Ethics and Corporate Policy, as reported in the *Toronto Star*.

Nitkin cited increasing firings and layoffs that overlook seniority and work history. He predicted business ethics will continue to skid with the slipping economy. Deteriorating practices, propelled by the pursuit of profits at any cost, will give rise to more court cases. Suits will focus on wrongful dismissals, environmental harms, shoddy products, workplace accidents and stress-related absenteeism.

There can be little doubt that economic insecurity sets off a domino effect, knocking down one pillar of psychological strength after another. Unable to afford even basics in the consumer heaven she or he witnesses every day, the individual questions the affordability of the culture's values. Principles become the prerogative of those who can afford the cost of living. So too, socially accepted behaviour.

And in a society that holds individuals responsible for their success no matter what conditions prevail, losses make no sense, other than a sense of personal failure. Gone are self-reliance, independence and access to rites of participation. The loss of mastery can manacle hope. And once hope slips beneath memory, so too may the individual's former moral code. Poverty, in lethal alliance with dashed dreams, conspires to depress not only the values of its individual victims, but also of the society as a whole.

Evidence of the downward ethical spiral is mounting. The recent report from the Canadian Mental Health Association (CMHA) links high unemployment with heightened rates of spouse and child abuse, sexual assault, and lawlessness, especially juvenile crime. Police statistics confirm that gratuitous violence during the commission of robberies is soaring. The press recite the bad news about children: increasing numbers have been coming into state care since the 1990 onset of the recession. Children's Aid Societies report a climbing incidence of depression and behaviour problems in children as families fracture under the strain of unemployment.

Every day foodbankers see the human wreckage from severe economic stress. Both Jill van Dijk in Vancouver and John Kinloch in Montreal have noticed the same trend: fathers, especially new immigrants, cannot cope with the shame of not being able to adequately house and feed their families. Humiliated, they abandon the home and sink into alcoholic sloth, even though they were not previously problem drinkers. Kinloch says he's been "greatly struck" by the deterioration in people who want to contribute but who are denied opportunities.

Many foodbankers condemn the way Canada welcomes new immigrants. They fault government for making a naturally tough transition needlessly tougher. Foodbankers, who meet newcomers daily, hear their frustrations: the language training they crave, but beyond a minimum cannot access; the prohibitions against working; the lack of supports in adjusting to a culture different from their homelands'. People are eager for and capable of self-sufficiency, but they end up demoralized and in foodlines.

A SPATE OF contemporary studies draws grim conclusions about the mounting social costs of poverty. The research shows more victims freighted with more complex problems and denser despair. A chasm now separates the world of the poor from the non-poor child. The latest report from the House of Commons Subcommittee on Child Poverty details the devastating impacts: health problems that begin before birth; unusually high rates of aggression, hyperactivity and delayed development; a dropout rate more than double the average, and heightened risk of disability and premature death.

*Unequal Futures* reports that the death rate from all causes for Canadians under 20 is 56 per cent higher among lowest-income than among highest-income families. The report points to firetrap housing and other appalling living conditions as the primary killers. The study also explores the "social nature" of death among the poor, the stressors that trigger skewed homicide and suicide rates.

Other research shows how poverty damages physical health. The CMHA study on the impact of unemployment connects it with unusually high rates of lung and heart diseases, and cirrhosis of the liver. The CMHA says that chronic stress seems to predispose people to certain infectious diseases and to cancer.

The weight of evidence linking poverty with stunted life chances is simply overwhelming. No body of evidence contradicts, or even mutes, the dangers research has confirmed and reconfirmed and elaborated since the Senate Committee issued its first poverty report over 20 years ago.

Failings of the social-security system, and of welfare in particular, consistently crop up as major contributors, not alleviators, of the pressures splintering so many lives. Respect for the system has sunk so low that even some insiders condemn it. For example, consider this excerpt from "How the Poor Will Survive," a discussion paper on Nova Scotia's public-assistance system, from the province's association of social workers:

> The present system produces malnutrition, hunger, illness, evictions, homelessness, school failures, conflict with the law etc. Individuals and families are suffering to the breaking point. This financial and social stress is picked up and reverberates for years in the health system and hospitals, in schools, in the courts and legal systems, in the penal system, in social agencies and institutions, in churches and charity groups. The long-term suffering, social costs and long-term economic costs to society are immense.

The price tag is staggering. Over the next 20 years, almost 200,000 teenagers will drop out of school because they are too poor to attend. The Subcommittee on Poverty says Canada will spend $1.3 billion in unemployment and welfare benefits, and will lose $7.2 billion in income taxes. If these students finished school, they'd earn an estimated $23 billion more.

Poverty's reach is long. It casts a shadow over a lifetime and a storm cloud over the land. And unless winds of change soon sweep through this country, the forecast looks bleak.

# V
# Shutdown Foodbanks or Privatize Pogey?

*It is good and right that we reach into the river of despair and rescue people who are drowning. But it is time to move upstream and see who is throwing them in.*
—Anonymous, from a Catholic Church newsletter in Manitoba

MEMBERS OF THE foodbanking movement are neither riven by differences nor welded together by a shared set of beliefs. Certainly the traditional link between church and charity still holds sway in the movement—more so than in most voluntary quarters. But the influence of churchy ideas does not mean foodbankers are cut from a single ideological cloth. Indeed, foodbanks attract people from a range of backgrounds and persuasions.

If all of them agree on nothing more, they believe in one thing: feed the hungry. And do it by moving provisions as efficiently and humanely as possible. Many of them also insist that moving against poverty is just as important. Within these broad agreements, differences abound. Most reduce into quibbles about method. Some expand into substantial debates.

In the method corner, for example, consumer-controlled models square off against charitable designs. In old-fashioned *noblesse oblige* charities, "haves" help "have-nots." Givers typically construe their deeds as a handup, while recipients often construe them as handouts to keep them down. Today, many poor people, fed up with the humiliations of charity, insist on managing their own betterment. Against stunning odds, like no cash and no clout, they pull together small, neighbourhood ventures to provide basics, particularly food and clothing.

Self-help differs dramatically from classical charity. The help-myself approach puts the consumer in command. The help-you approach puts the non-consumer, usually professionals and so-called experts, on top. The superior/inferior, powerful/powerless relationship reinforces historically potent myths that help trap the poor "in their place."

But, don't misunderstand. Foodbankers and anti-poverty activists do not hotly debate the merits of self-provisioning versus charity. Practitioners of bottom-up and top-down approaches agree that foodbanks fail to address the fundamental question of human rights, and of Canada's particular social-security guarantees. They agree that foodbanks, no matter who steers them, don't end hunger or fundamentally challenge poverty. Besides, few food programs are purely expert- or consumer-run. Service users work on governing boards and in the frontlines of many charities, irrespective of which model dominates. Even if foodbanks were run entirely by recipients—doubtless an improvement over the current norm—society would still rely on the voluntary sector to feed people. And that's what most foodbankers oppose.

## What's Wrong with Charity?

WITHIN THE FOODBANK movement, charity and justice clash. Some people contend the two are compatible. But most conclude charity prevails where justice is denied. Ask staff at Vancouver's End Legislated Poverty (ELP) what's wrong with charity and their answers echo the typical litany of condemnations. For starters, charity lets governments off the hook. It helps them dodge their legislated and moral duties to the people.

For another thing, charity creates a relationship of power and dependence rather than of equality and respect. The giver feels good about doing good, while the receiver feels diminished. Besides, the natural authority of the giver-getter relationship lends itself to easy abuse. Charity almost inevitably feeds the ache of worthlessness gnawing at people even before they walk through the foodbank door. How true the cliché that there are no free lunches: handouts come at a price, and that price is dignity.

Another flaw: far from ending poverty, charity perpetuates inequality. Meanwhile, it creates the illusion that needs are being met. Most hungry people, ELP points out, fall through the cracks of the charitable network in any case. Every depot has its stories of people who seek aid only after going without food for several days. People starve themselves for a variety of reasons, not least of them the terrible choice between self-respect and a full stomach.

At best, charity is a hit-and-miss affair. Many communities don't have foodbanks. Even where they exist and the media advertises them, even when people swallow back pride and face down stigma, many can't get to the depots. Physical and mental disabilities, bad health and bad weather, childcare and transportation costs, the prospect of carrying bulky bags on the bus—these and other obstacles block people from getting the groceries they need.

Who can promise a trip to the foodbank will prove worthwhile anyway? Larders are sometimes stocked, sometimes bare. Fresh produce is occasionally available, more often not. Coveted commodities, particularly high-protein foods and dairy products, are often rationed. A trek to the depot offers no guarantee of formula for the baby.

One's destiny at the foodbank depends entirely on donors. Did individuals have the spare money, time and inclination to give this week? Did they go to the supermarket and buy groceries to stuff bags likely donated by that food chain? Or did donor fatigue set in? Did demand climb faster than food gifts? At Winnipeg Harvest, donations are up 50 per cent this year, but demand is up over 200 per cent.

What's available also depends on what local producers, distributors and retailers need to dump: maybe barbecue sauce or glazed donuts. After a recent visit to Daily Bread's warehouse, a Toronto journalist reported in *Eye* weekly that the 182,400 jars of chow-chow on site could "cover a giant hot dog stretching from the corner of Bathurst and Spadina to the planet Venus." Cute? Perhaps. But it wasn't cute if you were a comer that week not keen on mustard relish.

One week's excess of relish can turn into next week's mustard famine, replaced perhaps by a Froot Loop feast. There's no telling. This is what you can predict: the typical hamper won't overflow with inviting comestibles. Aside from the nutritional insult many, but not all, contain, they often look unappetizing, loaded down with stale bread and wilted vegetables. Most make a mockery of Canada's food guide and subvert the premise of all half-decent social programs: the notion of national standards.

In a take-it-or-leave-it market, however, takers are stuck with foods they may not like, or with foods to which they or their children are allergic. Foodbanks cannot cater to personal preferences and dietary habits. They cannot respect ethnic menus or religious requirements. They cannot satisfy medically proscribed diets. To make matters worse, because of limited supplies, most foodbanks restrict consumer visits to once or twice a month. The typical hamper stretches three or four days.

Foodbankers are forever struggling to boost the nutritional value of their handouts. They also innovate programs to move quality food quickly. Trendsetting Second Harvest in Toronto, for instance, collects prepared leftovers from private and hotel parties and rushes them to agencies that feed the hungry. Clones of the idea have caught on in other cities. Foodrunners links Vancouver restaurants, caterers and bakeries with soup kitchens, missions and shelters. A donated, refrigerated truck races gourmet, perishable meals from what Jean Swanson at ELP calls "the tables of the rich to the tables of the poor."

Second Harvest and Foodrunners divert tons of food that would otherwise deluge dumpsters and litter landfills. The press enthuses about these New-Age organizations, billing them as perfect marriages between waste and a worthy cause. However slick these refinements, they remain refurbished charities with all their inherent ethical and practical problems.

## Should Foodbanks Close?

THE CONTENTION THAT charity prospers where justice loses out underlies yet another prickly problem—the issue of whether or not foodbanks should shut down. In the early 1980s, foodbanks saw themselves as necessary but temporary evils of a devilish economic downturn. But as the 1980s drew to a close—hunger swelling, foodbanks booming—the movement began to examine itself. Would food depots ever be able to close, or were they here to stay? By staying open, were they making it easier for governments to back off from supplying the needy with essentials? Were they aiding and abetting the state's reckless slashing of the social net?

Halifax, 1989. The dilemma came to a head. The foodbank announced it intended to close in January, 1994. The media loved it. Great copy. Scads of local and national stories appeared. Debate heated up in other foodbanks across the country. Haligonians hated the idea. How could the foodbank abandon the hungry? Did anyone imagine governments would act to curb poverty if padlocking drove a hidden problem into public view?

No, no one imagined that, at least they don't imagine it now after reflection, says Dianne Swinemar, executive director of Halifax's foodbank. Geoff Regan, the board's public-relations person, agrees. Both recognize that if they close, a new charity, not government, will likely fill the void. Why? Because, Regan reckons, many people believe it's okay to handle hunger through handouts. And those who don't accept foodbanks as the solution, don't want anyone to go hungry as a result of efforts to force government action.

Overwhelmingly negative response greeted the closing announcement. The public probably didn't realize what the foodbank was trying to accomplish with its warning. It hoped to galvanize opinion and activity around ending the need for foodbanks. Most foodbanks across the country share that goal. They say they're in business to put themselves out of business.

In Halifax, the principals reshaped their threat into "the foodbank has a goal of closing" by 1994. Given a prerequisite of reduced need for free food, few regard the deadline as realistic. Still, some like Geoff Regan think the gamble has been worthwhile. It highlighted the hunger crisis and the need for community action.

"I'll have none of that!" fumes Joan Turbitt at Community Unity, Burlington, Ontario's user-controlled foodbank. "People who propose shutting down aren't hungry." Members of End Legislated Poverty in Vancouver came to the same conclusion. ELP directors wrestled last year over calling for immediate closure. Executive director Jean Swanson says that non-users favoured shutdown, while users said "even though we hate foodbanks and are humiliated by them, they should stay open for now."

The stay-open-or-close-down debate predates the Halifax episode. Pierre Legault, originator and first manager of Moisson Montreal, recalls this "living-room argument" from the early days. "It's very comfortable for people to play with ideas while sitting in their living-rooms redoing the world. But when you're faced with a hungry person, we have to give food.... It's no solution to let people starve so that things get to an acute point where government *might* eventually do something. It's a callous position, I think, but for years we were beaten over the head by anti-poverty groups [taking this position]."

A minority still do maintain this stance. Last December, two former foodbank activists explained why in "Food Banks and the Politics of Hunger," in the *Canadian Forum*. Karen Shaver, who organized Second Harvest and served on Daily Bread's board, concluded that supporting foodbanks amounts to "directing community funds and resources to a destructive response."

Single-mother Carol Cayenne joined her Toronto housing-project neighbours in 1986 to set up Parents Against Poverty, a consumer-run food cupboard. By 1991, what Cayenne originally viewed as an "honourable thing" had for her and her co-organizers come to symbolize perpetuating poverty. They closed their depot and redirected their energies into finding alternatives to food charity.

SOME INSIDERS SAY all the heat steaming through the food-bank movement on the shutdown issue squanders precious energy and gets nowhere. They emphasize the question is not "Should foodbanks be abolished?" but rather "What role should they play?"

Graham Riches, author of *Food Banks and the Welfare Crisis*, summarized the now near-universal answer in a 1989 speech: "Food banks have to do more than simply collect food and disperse it ... they must both help individuals and work for reform and social change.... If they are to justify their continued existence, [they] must use their voluntary status to engage in the political struggle for the right of all members of Canadian society to have their basic needs fully met."

Foodbankers are free to get involved in politics, says Janet Hughes, longtime Edmonton board member. Because most operate, as a matter of principle, without much state funding, they can "go to bat" on issues of food and shelter. Many agree with Hughes that their financial independence positions them to fight hunger and want. Some foodbankers say they have a responsibility to lead that fight. Others say they have a stake in the struggle and a duty to contribute.

Marjorie Bencz, executive director of Edmonton's foodbank, is typical. Like many of her colleagues across the country, she highlights the credibility and community respect foodbanks have earned. And, she adds, with Canadians so wary of politicians, more people look to voluntary-sector leaders for solutions to social problems.

That, others say, translates into an opportunity. But to do what? To organize, and to participate in broad-spectrum, anti-poverty coalitions. Gerard Kennedy at Daily Bread in Toronto insists that the grassroots sector has to get organized. It must replace "seat-of-the-pants" coalitions with solid, broadbased ones capable of sustaining high-pressure campaigns. Kennedy thinks governments could be forced to guarantee income security if coalitions reflected diverse community interests rather than "just the usual suspects."

Many anti-poverty activists concur with Kennedy that the "usual suspects," meaning poor and other hardpressed populations, won't get very far going it alone. If voices of marginalized groups have never mattered much in the halls of power, they count even less now in these bottom-line times. Recognition is dawning, moreover, that the poverty problem isn't the private property of its victims. Rather, it belongs to the whole of society to solve.

Researchers who prepared *Getting to the Root of the Hunger Problem*, a recent update to the 1989 Regina hunger inquiry, interviewed workers in a spectrum of grassroots agencies. A consensus emerged from their comments: unless the larger community takes up the challenge of solving poverty, hunger is bound to worsen.

### Why Not Privatize Social Services?

DEBATES ABOUT THE future of foodbanking often rebound to two questions. Should foodbanks concede that they're here to stay, shuck off their shaky future as voluntary organizations and come under the state-run welfare umbrella? Or should they decry permanence and absorption into the bureaucracy, and instead soldier on, handing out food while simultaneously fighting poverty?

Naturally, people question the possibility of finessing a finale to food charity from inside the system. Some insist it's possible; others say "never." In the *Canadian Forum*, former fan turned foe Karen Shaver claims that "foodbanks have chosen their answer to poverty and that answer is to hand out food."

Her charge resonates in one current—probably a minor trend, it's hard to gauge—that whispers here and there across the country. Logic in that undercurrent runs like this: voluntary organizations operate more efficiently, with less bureaucracy and more humanity than government equivalents. Why not formally adopt parts of public welfare, through government contracts, and do a better job for less money?

Eldon Anderson, who chairs the board of Regina's foodbank, thinks "bigger and better NGOs"—non-governmental organizations—are part of the solution to poverty. Glen Pearson, head of the Ontario Association of Food Banks, goes much farther. Pearson, who also manages the London foodbank, accepts privatization of social services as inevitable, and not necessarily a bad thing. "If we want to do the best we can for the less fortunate, we can't just talk about social justice, we also have to talk about fiscal responsibility," he says.

Pearson thinks fiscally savvy, forwardlooking foodbankers should concentrate on better gleaning. Certainly, his fellow foodbankers share his concern with waste. Indeed, some of them question production and pricing policies, and the very nature of an economic system that dumps perhaps as much as a fifth of the food it produces. But, unlike Pearson, most don't regard better management of so-called surpluses as a primary solution to hunger. If good times return—good enough to finish the need for funnelling food—they hope foodbanking won't have any future. By contrast, Pearson thinks the movement should champion redistribution of "surplus" food as a long-term solution to hunger.

He wants foodbankers to collaborate with food industry and government powerbrokers. Together, they would mastermind efficient collection and delivery of food slated for waste. Pearson's plan dovetails nicely with social-spending cutbacks governments coast to coast are aggressively implementing. It also complements efforts by Ontario's minister of community and social services to encourage industry to donate cosmetically substandard food to agencies that serve the poor.

Pearson wants that food delivered, not to food depots, but to organizations like the Salvation Army with a tradition of direct-feeding programs. He reckons reliable free food will save effort and money the agencies normally spend begging or buying supplies. Then foodbankers could push these same services to allot their newfound money and staff time to mount "development projects"—like, for example, job training.

What if Pearson's plan sells? What if streamlining recycling into a fine art takes over as foodbanking's preferred direction? Soup kitchens will probably proliferate beyond their current glut. If the system guarantees groceries, then government incentive to guarantee decent welfare rates and wages may drop even further. Canada could find itself annexed even more to the U.S. way of welfare. Hence, poor people will have no choice but to patronize public kitchens. Foodbanks will become what they are already on the brink of becoming: a new bureaucracy to supplement below-subsistence wages and welfare.

Pearson agrees that better gleaning and distribution will spawn more food programs. But, along with a minority of his colleagues, he accepts governments' claim that they cannot do much about poverty. What governments can do, Pearson says, is act as visionaries for the voluntary sector. He wants the state to set national performance and accountability standards for private services. He and some others think it's high time foodbanks and governments partnered up. They should work out the details of what is effectively a takeover, by charities, of a parcel of government social-welfare functions.

OTHERS BRISTLE AT such suggestions. Privatization is the problem, not the solution, according to Doug Sabourin, executive director of Vancouver's Association of Neighbourhood Houses and a local foodbank boardmember. "Some voluntary organizations have been suckered into taking on contracted-out statutory government services."

New Brunswick communities have been delivering such services since 1983. That's when the province became the first one, and so far the only one, to join forces officially with food charities. The deal obliges those foodbanks, which choose to sign on, to feed the hungry, including people referred by welfare caseworkers. In return, the government agrees to partially finance foodbank operations.

One who believes it's a bad deal is Mike Gendron, involved in foodbanking from its inception, and now head of the Bathurst Volunteer Centre in New Brunswick. Contracting out lets the province buy a cheap dumping ground for needy families it refuses to help. Last year, Gendron's food programs helped 1,457 different individuals, including 845 children. The effort cost $647,000, of which the province contributed $40,000. The Centre had to raise $15 for every government dollar it received.

Partnership has neither lessened dependence on community cash donations, nor cut down on the vagaries of foodbanking. What such pacts can do, Gendron warns, is undermine advocacy. "The threat is always over your head that if you step out of line, they'll pull the plug." It is rumoured the New Brunswick government intends, if not to pull the plug, to cutback its $1.2 million grant to foodbanks, an outlay that hasn't increased since 1983 despite rocketing poverty.

FOODBANKERS TUSSLE AMONG themselves about these issues. Most fear, few favour, the idea of their organizations, however redefined, becoming fixtures. They fence with governments about how the two sides will relate. Meanwhile, the three big parties jockey for the politically correct line on foodbanks. The Tories and Liberals hardly ever say anything about hunger. But when they do mention foodbanks, they vacillate, alternately applauding them and bemoaning the necessity of their existence. Federally, the NDP officially supports funding foodbanks until they are no longer needed.

Inside the movement, some who admit foodbanks self-perpetuate say they must buck that trend. According to Jill van Dijk at Vancouver's foodbank, principals in her organization concede that "we're part of the problem now, and we're not prepared to participate in that.... We've decided we have to set some limits ... because otherwise we will become absolutely entrenched."

In the bid to dislodge themselves, what should foodbanks be fighting for? That's the question.

# VI
# Foodbankers' Shopping List of Solutions

*As they mark the end of their first decade, the road before foodbanks
forks off in two directions. One is politically difficult, challenges
the status quo and leads ultimately to the end of foodbanks.
The other is paved with good intentions. It's time to choose.*
—Carolyn Jack, *Canadian Forum*

## Decent Jobs, Livable Wages and Lifelong Learning

FOODBANKERS REGARD WORK as a human right. That
partly explains why the Canadian Association of Food
Banks (CAFB) gave its support to a draft social charter
that enshrines employment and favourable work conditions as
rights. The idea of work as entitlement stands in stark contrast
to Ottawa's proposed social covenant, which may be pushed
through as part of the constitutional package. The covenant
denies economic and social rights, relegating them both to assurances of "reasonable access." It's noteworthy that the draft
charter backed by the CAFB and by 23 other organizations,
most of them national, voluntary, and representing a wide
berth of grassroots concerns, should differ fundamentally from
the official position.

Everyone deserves a job. Foodbankers believe that if government were committed to full employment, the state could
wrestle joblessness to all-time lows. If society is unable to
guarantee people with a living through work, then, foodbankers insist, government must guarantee a fail-safe social
net as backup.

The charter the CAFB supports states that "everyone has an equal right to well-being, including a right to ... a standard of living that ensures adequate food, clothing, housing, child care, support services and other requirements for the security and dignity of the person and for full economic participation in their communities and in Canadian society."

Beyond these two maxims—the individual's right to work, and the state's duty to adequately support anyone denied access to the right to work—foodbankers support a raft of reforms. Their demands contain a central irony: progress on any of them requires progressive political thinking and increased social spending, two essentials strangled by the brand of neoconservatism now in vogue.

On wages, foodbankers don't equivocate: minimums must be livable. At current levels, they rarely purchase a scrape-by living. That's why the working poor, already a huge presence, may soon make up the fastest-growing stream in the breadlines. Foodbankers are adamant that full-time wages earned by two workers in an average-size family must suffice for getting by. That means workers need to earn a base rate around 75 per cent of the average industrial wage.

Foodbankers invariably mention pay equity in tandem with low wages. It is intolerable, they say, that women earn about two-thirds of what men earn. Pay equity also dogs other populations over-represented among those forced to scrounge for food: ethnic and racial minorities, and aboriginal peoples in particular. In addition, foodbankers chastise governments for lame enforcement of equity laws, which, in some provinces, are too limp to begin with.

After livable and equitable wages comes better protection for part-time workers. Foodbankers favour tough labour laws to prevent employers from replacing full-timers with casual employees. And stringent restraints, they say, must be placed on employers to control abuses of temporary workers. Secure part-time jobs and benefit packages head the list of foodbankers' demands.

BECAUSE PEOPLE CANNOT earn unless their skills mesh with the market, upgrading always insinuates itself into the conversation. Training may be one of few things on which the rich and the poor agree these days. Such unanimity has not always been the case. Most people, presumably, always wanted the best education possible. But until the technological revolution, the business lobby was comfortable with Canada's rank as third most illiterate among industrial nations. Our low level of educational attainment didn't bother industry because it didn't need a highly skilled workforce. Things have changed, however, and now employers demand training. So do workers displaced by the restructured economy. And many welfare recipients, as always, would give anything for an education.

Some provincial governments have been creating new departments and programs, even signing a few cheques. For example, in the spring, federal and provincial officials announced two experiments worth $50 million in total for New Brunswick and British Columbia. Designed, they say, to graduate people from the welfare treadmill into the job market, the scheme supplements low wages while recipients gain work skills.

On the surface, it looks like a good three-way partnership between business, government and unemployed workers. But small demonstration projects don't easily fire foodbankers' hopes. Wary volunteers wonder whether these new initiatives will pass the litmus test: will they graduate large numbers of recipients from welfare to work? Or will they transfer people onto workfare? Training and ensuring jobs, foodbankers say, must lift people off pogey, not put corporations on it by subsidizing low wages.

If it's to transcend the taint of forcing the poor to accept scullery work in return for benefits, or for wages no higher than benefits, training will have to break with its past. It will have to include on-site daycare so single mothers can afford to get ahead. Most important, it will have to tie in with real jobs leading to real futures.

ONE IN FIVE Canadians—maybe as many as one in four—cannot read this sentence. Over 30 percent of high-school students across the country drop out. Another 10 per cent who hang in do not learn to read, write or handle numbers well enough to function in society. The now-defunct Economic Council of Canada warned that another 1 million kids will leave school during the 1990s unable to read or balance a chequebook.

True, during the past decade literacy finally crept onto government and business agendas. But small money and smaller thinking barely put a dent in the need. Now, training, particularly retraining of displaced workers, is overtaking the prominence adult basic education briefly enjoyed.

Foodbankers interact daily with adults desperate for chances at self-sufficiency. People on both sides of that exchange worry that the train-the-best-and-forget-the-rest mentality, which has plagued government and corporate literacy programs, will carry over into new training packages. It's no wonder worry runs so high. Business is suddenly hep on promoting a new miracle cure it calls educational "excellence." Foodbankers want to know: excellence for whom, and at what price? Does excellence mean more investment in the so-called brightest, usually from the best-off backgrounds?

In this decade, an estimated half of new jobs will require five years of postsecondary education combined with training. At the same time, an estimated 50 per cent of jobs—many requiring less than high school—lost to the ravages of recession, won't return. Workers who held those posts haven't a prayer of finding self-sustaining employment unless a bold new blueprint for lifelong learning, second-chance and second-career training draws them in.

Yet foodbankers cannot imagine excellence means more opportunities for the newly and especially for the chronically dispossessed. They fear governments will write off vast numbers of workers business no longer needs, refuses to retrain, and regards as disposable. They suspect this subtext lurks beneath Ottawa's willingness to forego national standards by surrendering training to the provinces. They worry the fanfare about excellence means the country is on the brink of installing a permanent caste of paupers.

### Adequate, Affordable Housing

BECAUSE OUTPRICED HOUSING combined with low incomes is the killing combination driving people into breadlines, foodbankers stress housing reform with a tone of urgency. They say the private market will never give low-revenue families a fair chance to put a decent roof over their heads. Indeed, the Canadian Association of Food Banks has found that when welfare rates rise, rents rise to match, making landlords the welfare system's primary beneficiaries. Most foodbankers would agree with Gisèle LeBlanc at Garde-Manger in Montreal when she charges that welfare is little more than a "direct deposit" system for landlords.

Hence, foodbankers favour both rent controls and assisted housing, two nonstarters on government agendas. Foodbankers say government must reverse its direction in both areas. Ottawa need not only reinstate cuts, but also initiate a creative housing policy to help exploding populations of need.

It must help homeless and precariously housed families straying in the streets. It must help women and children escaping violent men, but finding few affordable alternatives to their dangerous homes. It must help young workers who cannot afford a room of their own. And it must help forgotten psychiatric patients holed up in ramshackle rooms and in cardboard boxes.

Foodbankers also call for changes to zoning bylaws. Tens of thousands of city dwellers live in illegal basement or attic apartments, what realtors call "mother-in-law" suites. Everyone's afraid of getting caught, fined or evicted. Yet many homeowners need the income, just as renters need the rooms.

Social-class prejudices and economic self-interest anchor these laws in place. As foodbankers see it, City Hall entrenches class lines. It's been observed that one ratepayer is worth at least two rent-payers in battles with city councils. And one developer is worth a bus full of ratepayers. So, when vocal, single-family homeowners from midscale neighbourhoods oppose zoning changes that would attract downscale renters, homeowners usually win.

Some homeowners fear zoning liberalism because it paves the way for lowrises, group homes, conversions of single to multiple-family dwellings and higher density. Their key fear is sinking property values. But, on the positive side, re-zoning promotes inclusive neighbourhoods, housing that doesn't confine the poor to soul-destroying ghettos.

City councils normally resolve the conflict between relatively affluent and poor by cramming "mixed-use" housing into a few neighbourhoods "in transition," where gentrification competes with integration. Foodbankers say we can no longer accept this non-solution, which unduly burdens a few target neighbourhoods. That's why they've joined housing activists clamouring for government assistance to guarantee an adequate, affordable roof over every head.

### Income Security

FOODBANKERS THINK OF work as the cornerstone of income security. But they recognize that the right to work, now absent from our society, will not be realized overnight. Even if the right were implemented, for a variety of reasons not everyone could completely support themselves. Under all circumstances, foodbankers say public supplements must cover basic living costs. That, by definition, means indexing rates annually. Today, the various programs pay from 30 to 60 per cent below government's low-income cutoffs.

Aside from basement rates, "payday," as recipients call it, presents another big problem. Utility monopolies and landlords devour the money. The problem of unscrupulous landlords, who command as much as 60 to 70 per cent of welfare income, comprises one of the difficulties in defining how much assistance is enough. Foodbankers, however, aren't so flummoxed as officials. In addition to rent controls they'd fix welfare rates using a "market basket" approach—one which gauges consumer costs for essential goods and services, and pegs financial assistance accordingly.

But, at the moment, political commitment to a market-basket baseline languishes in the stratosphere. Therefore, welfare advocates are reduced to agitating for higher food allowances, and for emergency food vouchers. As public transit fares skyrocket—by March of this year, a single, one-way cash fare in Toronto cost $2!—advocates also demand reasonable transportation allowances, or transit passes for the poor. Many typical items on the advocates' list for the working poor—things like dental care, prescription eyeglasses, some prosthetic and assistive devices for people with disabilities—were axed during the frenzied cutbacks of the 1980s.

The cutback climate is hostile to an anti-poverty view of public assistance, such as the one expressed in *Transitions*, the report from Ontario's Social Assistance Review Committee. It describes welfare's goal as ensuring individuals "make the transition from dependence to autonomy and from exclusion on the margins of society to integration within the mainstream of community life."

Foodbankers witness the opposite. They meet people desperate to kick the dole, literally crying for education and work, choked off from opportunities by built-in disincentives. They see the psychological wear and tear on families forced to battle the system for their daily bread. They see how it crushes self-esteem. They see all the roadblocks to independence: work part-time and they hatchet your cheque, take a job and you lose your daycare subsidy or your transit pass, try to get ahead through education and they channel you into some dead-end training program, express an interest in college or university and they say secretarial training might be "more appropriate."

Christine Bengston in Edmonton has heard the latter phrase more than once. She is a single mom recently on welfare for the first time. She begged her caseworker for financial support to finish a college program she started prior to welfare. The worker refused, forcing Bengston to choose between a minimum-wage job and a sponsored secretarial course.

The welfare system may be better known for the dependence it breeds than for the assistance it offers. Foodbankers now watch helplessly as the psychology of defeat and dependence transfers from the cash lines to the chow lines. After a decade in the misery business, volunteers are now serving children from families they met 10 years ago. Today their kids need handouts for their own young families. The progeny of poverty inherit not one, but two welfare systems, one for their rent money, the other for their food.

TALK TO FOODBANKERS about welfare, and you end up talking about taxes. Tax talk invariably leads to two issues. The first: unfairness in the tax system. Even if a campaign for livable welfare rates were to succeed, foodbankers know those who can least afford it would be forced to foot the bill.

The second issue is a conundrum. On the one hand, foodbankers cite surveys showing Canadians want governments to tackle hunger and poverty. On the other hand, they remind us that people distrust how governments spend money. To compound the mess, the public disrespects the welfare system. People think sinking more dollars into it only enriches bureaucrats.

Ordinary people have circumnavigated this conundrum by creating a private welfare system. But, except for a minority of foodbankers who think charity is the way to go, most foodbankers know this is no solution.

The solution, as foodbankers envision it, is an empowering and accountable welfare system to replace the soul-destroying and wasteful bureaucracy now in place. This goal, however, demands two missing prerequisites: responsible government trusted by taxpayers, and an absolute commitment to ensuring everyone enjoys access to basic necessities.

Foodbankers more often regard the welfare system as poverty's handmaiden than its backbreaker. And even though many foodbankers have regular run-ins with welfare workers, it's uncommon to hear them blame caseworkers for the system's callousness. In fact, many sympathize with frontline workers. Given swollen caseloads and severe cutbacks, they say it's unreasonable to expect even the best professionals to practice "real social work." By that they mean helping people achieve independence and dignity.

That the welfare system urgently needs a makeover is the one current running through foodbankers' discussions of these matters. An essentially punitive model must be scrapped—tinkering won't do—in favour of a model that truly enhances the lives of those on both sides of the counter.

SOME FOODBANKERS THINK the solution to income security lies in a guaranteed annual income—a 1960s invention with right-wing American roots. Canadian policymakers are now eyeing it with new affection. On the surface, the GAI sounds seductive. But dig a little, and you unearth many suspicions. Even enthusiasts fret about what form it might take, and how little money it might put in the hands of the needy.

Some anti-poverty activists smell a rat. They worry because considerable evidence points to GAI upcoming on the federal government's agenda. If it suits the neoconservative penchant for privatization and cutbacks, they reckon it can't bring good to the people. British Columbia sociologist Dennis Guest, in his book *The Emergence of Social Security in Canada*, contends the GAI will entrench an underclass here similar to the mass of poor workers in the United States. Lise Corbeil at the National Anti-Poverty Organization expects the GAI is coming and that it will take the form of direct subsidies to industry for low wages.

If the speculators are right, taxpayers will, in effect, foot the bill for starvation wages. Some fear the 1992 federal budget, which delivered a few dollars to the working poor and nary a penny to the unemployed poor, foretold what's in the works—consigning a strata of workers to paltry wages taxpayers will top up to subsistence level.

Fears that government intends to further abandon people the welfare system writes off as "unemployable," along with the unemployed but work-ready, routinely surface in chats with foodbankers. They expect the working poor will receive a few new crumbs, possibly through a GAI-type scheme. But they

also suspect that rate freezes and cutbacks, which further pauper-
ize the worst-off, will subsidize those crumbs. Sinking one layer
of the poor lower to raise another a titch—could this, they wonder, forewarn a developing trend?

### Universal Childcare

DAYCARE ENJOYS SUCH prominence in public consciousness that Mulroney made it a plank in his bid to
retain power. He called childcare the "centrepiece" of
his social program. On August 11, 1988, the Prime Minister
told Parliament: "I believe a decade hence, the Canada Child
Care Act will be regarded as perhaps the most important social
innovation of the 1980s.... Child care will be regarded by all
Canadians as a fundamental right." Until 1992, he periodically
punctuated speeches with a renewed pledge to a massive program. When the finance minister finally dropped the axe on
the "fundamental right" this year, it was little wonder people
reacted cynically.

Foodbankers are still trying to decode the broken promise. Is
government determined to drive women out of the workforce, as
it did after World War II, to make way for jobless men? Or is it
simply trying to keep unemployed females at home? Is no daycare an insurance policy for employers who depend on part-time
women workers? Without childcare, many mothers have no
choice but to juggle the bad jobs that help keep profits healthy
and families hungry.

Far from letting up, the critical need for childcare is intensifying. *The Canadian Family in Crisis* reports that over half of the total
workforce needs daycare. Statscan figures show that mothers of
about 3 million children under age 12 are working. But, by 1990,
according to the *Globe and Mail*, the country had only 321,000 li-
censed daycare spaces.

Need is so great that even the concept of childcare is expanding.
Daycare isn't enough any more. Declining moral values and
mounting violence put more kids at risk of ruin. Hence, after-
school supervision now factors into the task of taking care of kids

outside their homes. And just as the need for childcare reaches an acute stage, government retrenches, announcing its exit from the daycare stage.

## School Lunches

TEACHERS OFTEN FIND themselves trying to cope with overcrowded classes in under-resourced schools. It's hard to help hyper kids, ricocheting around the room, stick to their seats let alone catch onto new ideas. Listless youngsters, sleepy after a sugar-coated breakfast—or no breakfast—don't make star pupils either.

Teachers grapple for ways to cope. Grade One teacher Monique Desmarais at Hochelaga Elementary explained in the *Montreal Gazette* her method for scheduling exams. For two years, she tested kids twice a month, once at the beginning, then at the end. Pupils consistently scored better on the first test. Why? Because, she discovered, they ate better early in the month when the welfare cheque arrived.

Not surprisingly, teachers and their unions often favour the quickest fix—school feeding programs—quicker, that is, than the prospect of injecting money into poor families.

But, just how serious is hunger among school children? In a 1990 public-health survey of Toronto principals, 28 per cent identified hunger as a problem. Since then, the Toronto Board of Health has endorsed a $65-million-a-year blueprint to feed every school child once a day. Hunger is serious enough that last year Quebec's ministry of education announced a $1-breakfast and $2-lunch subsidy for 20 per cent of schoolkids, about 20,000 pupils in 67 targeted schools. The plan requires parents to contribute 75 cents a day. It also leans on voluntary organizations to collect, prepare and serve the food. Hunger is serious enough that earlier this year, the British Columbia government inaugurated a $7-million lunch program in schools with clusters of needy kids.

Although school meals spur controversy, many foodbankers support them. They see that provincial governments more readily embrace school lunch programs than proposals to help cash-strapped parents feed their own children. Schemes for feeding kids outside their homes are not new. *Children, Schools and Poverty*, a 1989 report from the Canadian Teachers' Federation, points out that many schools have long run informal "sharing shelves," even catered programs. Funding comes from school boards, governments and charities. Service organizations, also reliant on eclectic funding arrangements, host breakfast clubs and free lunches in community settings.

Besides precarious funding, another drawback plagues these programs: social stigma. Advocates argue that without universal programs—meaning programs for all kids in designated schools —free food will always inflict a sting. But ideally, grabbing a bite at school won't invite any more notice than going home for lunch.

But what some regard as a dream, others view as a nightmare. Last year the *Globe and Mail* quoted Jean-Yves Desgagnés, coordinator of Montreal's Common Front of Recipients of Social Assistance. School breakfasts are "better than children starving but the public has to realize it's an act of gross hypocrisy.... What are these kids supposed to do all summer? They're hungry now and they have to wait until September for a free breakfast, and we're supposed to be thankful? I'm sorry, but that's a scandal."

"Scandalous" is a word that often crops up around this issue. John Kinloch, spokesperson for the CAFB, and executive director of Montreal's Multi Caf community cafeteria, lathers at the mention of school lunches. "The [Quebec] government made all these pious statements about ... hunger in the schools.... There's been this big push for family policy, the whole *'intégrité de la famille québécoise.'* Well, if they were concerned ... why don't they just give parents the money to feed their own children?"

Kinloch underlines the ironies. Government slashes welfare, then pours a pittance into school lunches. Through "participation programs," it hires parents, whose cheques have been cut, to make sandwiches for their own kids. It's an "absolutely ridiculous" situation, says Kinloch.

In *Poor Children in Ontario Schools,* the Federation of Women Teachers outlines many common objections to school feeding. The embarrassment factor. The exclusion of other family members also suffering from hunger. The stopgap nature of such programs. And, most worrisome, the risk that school meals will become permanent. *Children, Schools and Poverty* adds to the list of woes the erosion of parental responsibility that the school as free restaurant implies. The report concludes that "like foodbanks, school food programs may provide bandaids that work against rather than for long-term solutions."

## Advocacy and Self-Help

FORCE FOODBANKERS TO choose cure-alls that beat out other contenders in the struggle against hunger, and most will mention advocacy and self-help. These words carry a lot of baggage. Advocacy usually refers to one-on-one befriending. An advocate connects with a repeat foodbank user. Ideally a welfare "survivor" herself, the advocate helps the ground-down consumer assess escape hatches. Is there any way out of the welfare snare? If not, as is most often the case, is there a way to shimmy up a notch or two?

Help may mean referral to other services. Often it amounts to combing the recipient's welfare stubs for underpayment. Or alerting the person to emergency aid the system sometimes permits but frequently "forgets" to mention. Advocacy, then, often involves watchdogging, making it a little tougher for the system to cheat. Advocates often intervene with a caseworker or supervisor. Intervention may lead to a review that nets more money. Sometimes advocates back up recipients in face-to-face battles with the system.

Alongside advocacy and its spinoffs, foodbanks sponsor or inspire a mindboggling array of self-help projects. Although the term "self-help" implies complete consumer control, in many instances volunteer professionals or paid facilitators play key roles. But whatever form these projects take, their aim of empowering consumers unites them.

It's fair to call "empowerment" *the* food charity buzzword. Indeed, the desire to support individuals' power to control their own lives fans out beyond foodbanks far into the voluntary sector. This new enabling focus is a reaction to crushing losses in quality of life and in self-esteem that beneficiaries of our so-called helping systems suffer.

Foodbankers hope that a strengthened inner core, bred through self-help successes, will embolden individuals to fight for a better deal. Some imagine a restored sense of personal potency will lead not only to enhanced individual lives, but to collective betterment.

Among self-help projects, community kitchens curry the most favour. The idea was imported from South America where collective buying and cooking caught on in the slums during the 1970s. It took hold in Montreal in the late 1980s. Since then, the concept has spread across the country.

Andrée Ménard, director of Promis, a Montreal service for immigrants and refugees, and Eileen Sheridan, project coordinator, describe how their kitchens work. They draw participants from Montreal's densely-populated Côte des Neiges district. Usually three or four women, who need to cook for a combined total of say 12 adults and children, join a French, English, Spanish or Arabic-speaking collective. Each member contributes $2 a month for each family member. The project subsidizes every $2 with $3. In addition, Promis stocks its kitchen with bulk-bought basics.

The women meet twice a month. The first time they exchange recipes, plan menus, divvy up the kitty and assign shopping. The second time they cook a week's worth of take-home dinners.

Some community kitchens depend on a volunteer, a paid nutritionist or a staff coordinator. The consumers themselves run others. Some kitchens buy their cooking supplies, while others stock their pantry for free at the local foodbank. But no matter what variations, collective kitchens share common ambitions: cut costs, boost nutrition, bolster self-reliance, reduce social isolation and restore a sense of community.

Gardening and preserving for the same aims is also gaining ground. And like collective kitchens, community gardens encompass a plethora of models: balcony and backyard growing experiments, group-cultivated plots, and everything from vegetable canning to jam-making jamborees.

Do projects like these make a difference? Yes, and no. John Pasquini at Moisson Montreal zeroes in on the confidence-building factor. But even the biggest fans of self-help admit to its limitations. Former welfare advocate Lorelee Manning, who now directs Regina's Council on Social Development, describes these ventures as "part of empowering people to discover their roles in society and community. But, alone they are insufficient. Change has to be something everyone has a stake in." Self-help represents "hopeful totems" says Gerard Kennedy of Toronto's Daily Bread. Projects offer up tangible results against a backdrop of stagnant social policy.

Lise Corbeil at the National Anti-Poverty Organization is more skeptical. She criticizes schemes that rely on professional direction rather than on consumers. She rates collective kitchens and their cousins, even if user-run, as bit players on the anti-poverty stage. Corbeil reminds us that projects typically target better budgeting, when the real issue is lack of money. Sue Cox, a veteran of U.S. foodbanking, makes the most important point: every new service foodbanks add reduces the pressure on government to deal with poverty.

## Conclusion

JOINING THE FOODBANK movement is not like joining a religious movement. Among foodbankers there is one non-contestable article of faith—feed the hungry here and now, don't wait for them to inherit the earth. But no other fixed dogma draws adherents together. Besides "feed the poor," a second canon unites many: "Fell poverty." To help banish want and to empower individuals, foodbankers regard consumer control, self-help and advocacy as sacrosanct. Beyond this scripture, a few debates and many agreements abound.

Debates often focus on the future of foodbanking. But after more than a decade of brisk business, though loath to admit it, the majority of foodbanks seem resigned to semi-permanence. Most favour the status quo: partial to full independence. If the welfare mill absorbs them, they fear it will smother their voice as public educators, critics and advocates. That integration will entrench food charity once and for all is their greatest fear.

A small minority think foodbanks should quit pretending they're temporary. They should embrace governments as partners. A new team, with players from the state, the voluntary sector and the food industry, should share the field. The team's aim: efficient management of food slated for waste. Solve hunger, and save tax dollars, by moving "surpluses." Formally convert food charity into a wing of the welfare system.

No matter where they stand philosophically, most foodbankers share the same shopping list of necessities. The broader anti-poverty movement, indeed many people calling for social reform and progress, have for a long time posted a similar list.

It starts with good jobs, living wages, pay equity and decent working conditions—all protected by tough, enforceable laws. It adds training and adult education, to unshackle ignorance and to open a world of literacy, skills and opportunities.

It goes on to the need for assisted, affordable, appropriate housing. It calls for prohibitions against landlords gouging poor people's incomes. The list champions livable welfare rates. It seeks supports, in place of existing discouragements, for recipients to help themselves. It mentions real social work. Unlike much government-sponsored casework of today, real social work assists people in achieving dignity and power over their lives.

Daycare—high calibre, low cost, accessible and universal— makes the list as well. Without it, foodbankers foresee worsening poverty thwarting single mothers and young families. So many kids are so hungry that controversial school feeding programs appear on the list as well.

Also making the list is a hodgepodge of new services designed to plug holes in the crumbling wall of social security. These initiatives address human suffering, particularly from drugs, alcohol, and from various forms of social violence. They also embrace more culturally sensitive and coordinated services for new immigrants.

The list doesn't end here; it goes on to support a draft social charter which would provide a constitutional underpinning for economic and social renewal.

Perhaps this package somewhat appeases foodbanking's critics. But even within the movement's network of friends, some, like Lorelee Manning at Regina's Council on Social Development, say progress cries out for louder, more determined voices. "People ... have a voice they have to use, not just for their own lives, but for society." Because if foodbankers do not sound louder alarm bells, who will?

# VII
# Justice—Not Charity

*Are we ready to stand up to the forces in our own societies that deprive people of food, even indirectly? The right to food and the freedom to resist injustice are inseparable. There is no freedom without bread, and no bread without freedom.*
—Susan George, *Ill Fares the Land*

WHICH IDEALS EVOKE Canada, not as it is today, but as it is supposed to be? Democratic? Independent? Peace-loving? Justice-minded? Defender of human rights? Protector of vulnerable citizens? These watchwords resonate because, presumably, most of us want to renovate this land using building blocks made from these elusive qualities. Judging from foodbankers' comments and from public outcry, it is safe to assume the majority reject the blueprint for this country drawn up by our governments and their corporate bedfellows.

Their Canada is built on democracy for the few. It is built on sellout to foreign conglomerates, on slavering to the U.S., on doing America's bidding in its international political and military adventures. And it is built on vast disparities, now growing vaster than ever, in income and in access to health, education and social services.

Ordinary people disdain developments that increasingly pockmark the country with pinpoints of super wealth and craters of super poverty. They object to living in a pressure sandwich: members of the thin uppercrust commanding an ever-bigger bite, the majority on desperate tenterhooks in the middle, and the ever-thicker sludge of the bottom layer threatening to absorb them. They oppose the expansion of poverty and the retraction of social protections. They spurn the powerhouses that create

113

conditions for homelessness. And they refuse to accept that anyone in Canada should have to subsist on substandard food discarded by transnationals.

Foodbanks symbolize many things gone wrong. But above all they signal triumph for those who would fill their own larders by emptying everyone else's. Foodbanks testify to stunning achievements by the monied in making themselves the repo men of rough times. And when we load up our little care packages for food charities, we are dupes of those who offload the economic crisis onto people who had nothing to do with its creation.

The make-the-people-pay plan works because the majority, who desire economic and social justice, do not press the levers of power. They do not have the clout to enact or enforce policies to protect the poor, or everyone else, from the unfettered freedoms of the rich. A case in point: the North American Free Trade Agreement. Mulroney's own polls show that over 70 per cent of the population opposes NAFTA. Where, then, did Trade Minister Michael Wilson get the mandate, never mind the moxie, to dare sign such a deal? On whose say-so and for whose benefit did he negotiate?

An old lesson emerges with renewed clarity from the NAFTA scandal: ordinary citizens do not call the shots. They receive, or are denied, economic and social blessings at the whim of those who claim to act on their behalf. NAFTA is just one of many reminders that we need enforceable, justiciable guarantees of rights.

Yet economic and social rights for individuals are conspicuously absent from the constitutional compromise the old boys finessed this summer. Amid all the rhetoric about a social covenant, as if its inclusion in the deal were a great coup for social progress, no one mentions that the terms are non-binding. The economic and social union clauses depend on governments' goodwill, possibly augmented by toothless watchdog agencies. Unenforceable promises of reasonable access replace what ought to be entrenched rights.

The proposals do not guarantee the right to a livelihood, through work or social transfers, consistent with a broadly accepted level of well-being. Moreover, judging by media reports of the *in camera* horse trading, the fatal omission of rights was a

114

non-issue. Rather, the Senate, which many people regard as silly and irrelevant, commanded centre-stage in the save-the-country show.

The something-for-everyone but nothing-principled-for-anyone deal—except, notably, for aboriginal peoples—does not address the needs of Canada's neediest. The powerful brokered a shaky compromise that fiddles with the form of their power-sharing arrangements. But it bodes for little or nothing in the way of power and progress for various excluded populations, such as women and the poor.

Little wonder the constitutional draft is so botched. The brainchild of about a dozen suits bickering in backrooms as if our future were their private property, the product represents ther process and their priorities. It does not reflect a public consensus, achieved through democratic participation, of what Canadians deem fair and acceptable.

With the media at their disposal to incite narrow patriotism, according to which only enemies of Canada oppose the package, architects of the constitutional misfortune may get their way. Given a populace who've had it with the haggling, the premiers may succeed in bullying their constitutional overtures or some tinkered version of them past the public. And that may result in the almost deified goal of "keeping the country together," at least temporarily.

But, even if a national referendum endorses the deal, it will not resolve the eternally nagging question of Quebec's rights as a nation. Nor will it provide the dispossessed anywhere in the country with greater assurances of a livelihood than they enjoy today. The constitutional draft, whether it dies or flies, promises to have about as much effect on the breadlines and welfare rolls as the poor have on Brian Mulroney.

IN THE BOOM periods following each economic bust, the rate of joblessness never retreats to its pre-crisis point. After every downturn, unemployment levels off at a new high. Salesmen of the status quo then try to pitch the idea that the new high represents "normal" unemployment. They sell a spiral of sinking expectations.

Canadians have a lot to fear from the growing unemployment and poverty. Throughout the 1980s, joblessness held at over 7 per cent, the highest plateau reached in the 1970s. A decade earlier, 3 to 4 per cent unemployment was called "normal." The now-defunct Economic Council of Canada warned that following the current recession, unemployment could settle at 8 per cent. Doubtless, the hucksters of redefined "full employment" will peddle the idea that 8 or 9 per cent unemployment signals normalcy and economic health.

In the same vein, the powers that be regularly alter the snapshot of a good society. It used to be one in which the "welfare state" protected the poor from starvation and homelessness. One in which a range of social benefits were proffered on mid-range earners. One in which a significant minority of working-class kids could reasonably hope for a college education. One in which health care was relatively high quality and accessible to most everyone.

Now the growing notion of what's normal includes hunger and foodbanks, homelessness and shelters. It includes substantially reduced social benefits. It includes a creeping reality of postsecondary education as a preserve of the rich. It includes lesser healthcare and more user fees. Granted, the sales job on this distorted version of the desirable society hasn't won many converts. Nonetheless, the mind managers manipulate us into settling for a world that, for the majority, means a place increasingly revised for the worse. For the privileged few, however, it means quite the opposite.

The term "mind managers" does not suggest any conspiracy. The powerful don't need to connive, as U.S. education critic and author Jonathan Kozol points out. They have what Kozol calls a "systemic conspiracy" automatically working for them. It kicks in without invidious intervention. The Persian Gulf war and the North American Free Trade Agreement illustrate Kozol's point.

Ottawa did not have to collude with Lord Thompson or Gérard Veilleux or other media magnates to ensure favourable treatment of these outrages, apparently opposed by most Canadians. The monopoly media reflexively knew what was required of them, and they did it, no questions asked. Day in and day out, they awarded prime time and prime space to the warmongers, and, until the deal was signed and all hell broke loose, to the pro-NAFTA politicians, especially Michael Wilson.

During the war, they buried dissent in occasional brave little documentaries and quick commentaries. They contained opposition to NAFTA in a sprinkling of news-story references and in letters to editors. On both of these issues, the media used the top of the news and front-page headlines to express the official line. Thereby, they created the impression, especially on the war, that no other significant positions existed. NAFTA reporting was more balanced, but hardly representative of the true balance of pro and anti forces.

Kozol says the whole system is rigged to render what amounts to a "conspiracy of effect." He uses these phrases to describe how the U.S. maintains an education system riven by race and social-class differences. But his characterization applies as well to the broader political setup both in the States and in Canada.

MANY DANGERS LURK in a society whose "progress" is marked by losses. One danger lies in the temptation to fight back only to regain what's been taken away. Another rests in the enticement to measure progress against a memory of the past, often idealized, or against a low standard in some other country. These seductions distract us from measuring Canada's advance against a bold vision of a fundamentally better future.

If you examine, for instance, foodbankers' shopping list of solutions in the previous chapter, what do you find? Most items call for the return of stolen benefits, such as reinstatement of housing cutbacks. Or they call for a realization of broken promises, such as the national daycare program. Perfectly legitimate demands.

Indeed, just about everyone fighting poverty and decrying cutbacks supports most of the foodbankers' solutions. And well we should.

There's a "but" however. As farfetched as it seems at this moment, just suppose the protest movement wins its demands. Under the prevailing setup, who will pay for better wages and welfare? For daycare and medicare? Indeed, for everything on the list? Costs will be passed on, in the form of regressive taxes and price hikes, to the broad public. They will not be disbursed throughout the population according to ability to pay.

Other problems arise when protest concentrates only on reclaiming losses. However unwittingly, because of the bleak present, we tend to prettify the past. Many of the anti-Tory tirades so popular today in books and magazines, although they don't claim it outright, hint that things were hunkydory before Mulroney took over. Nostalgia for the good old days blurs memory of what were, in fact, bad old days—not as grim as these days perhaps, but not exactly a dream world of socioeconomic justice and national independence.

We seem always to define ourselves in relation to romanticized bygone days, or in relation to a worse scenario elsewhere. In Canada, that means constant crosschecking with Uncle Sam who dictates our politics, our economy and our culture. America, however, is a rotten basis for comparison. Even putting aside its grotesque machinations as the world's self-proclaimed gendarme, the U.S. furnishes the worst example of domestic decency among industrial countries. With its unrestrained moneygrubbers, perishing middle class and bursting ghettoes, it hardly merits mention as a model. With its threadbare social programs, exorbitant and exclusive healthcare system, and its rich/poor schools, it can only be considered a standard-bearer of injustice.

Rather than applaud Canada for bettering the American nightmare, perhaps it's time to divine our own dreams. Maybe the moment has arrived to start measuring our forward march against a new vista of what Canadians want. Conceivably, the time is ripe to seize our sovereignty, now in the hands of Parliament and the

118

Queen, and create a constituent assembly through direct and universal suffrage.

From the outset of the constitutional fracas, ordinary people clamoured to participate, to make sure that what mattered to them made it onto the agenda. Ottawa responded by stage-managing and hobbling the public role. Ultimately, it completely excluded the people—and their agenda items. Now, perhaps, as the unsatisfactory results of secret deals struck behind closed doors come into public view, people will insist on hammering out an acceptable constitution themselves. A bill of rights and responsibilities made by everyday people for themselves. Not made in the boardrooms and backrooms by and for domestic and foreign moneybags.

WHAT STANDS IN the way? An ossified electoral and political system at odds with the popular demand for democracy. A system stalemated by partisan politicking. A system uninterested in and incapable of solving the country's urgent problems. When was the last time you felt all members of federal or provincial parliamentary houses were pulling together to tackle a crisis, say unemployment for example? Did you ever feel they were motivated by a desire to score gains for the people, rather than to score political advantages for their parties?

Seeing how crippled the political system has become makes one wonder whether the partisan paradigm has outlived its usefulness. It makes one question whether any political parties ought to run the country. Perhaps we'd be better off if parties had to lobby for their policies from outside Parliament.

Seeing how deadlocked the system has become makes one yearn for a new model with some very unusual features. Features such as representatives who reflect the makeup and the outlook of the population. As some foodbankers ask, can we continue to allow white, male professionals, mostly rich lawyers and businessmen from privileged backgrounds, to dominate power?

Features such as ongoing accountability, with grassroots voters having the right and the means to recall reps who fail to satisfy them. As some foodbankers ask, can we continue to accept sham accountability? Is it okay if politicians construe their positions as *carte blanche* to do whatever they please until some distant election—when we get to replace them with a carbon copy?

Another feature, even farther from our collective experience and requiring considerable imagination: politicians driven, above all, by a commitment to untangling problems weighing down on ordinary people. Such dedication would mean turning things upside down, putting the public good before partisan ambitions. It would mean replacing the current overarching goal of grabbing or clinging to power with the goal of building a just and admirable society.

It seems unlikely that such a lofty ambition can be achieved in the context of our sick system in which three remarkably similar sets of players play musical chairs. Absurdity has reached such a pitch that if the media didn't attach party labels to the players, you probably couldn't guess their affiliation by their policies or practices.

But in the absence of enduring principles in any of the parties, other than pragmatism and opportunism, it's near impossible to know who will stand for what once they assume power. In the end, they all seem to stand for slight variations on the same old themes.

If you heard that one of the three wanted to scrap the Senate while the other two opposed getting rid of it, to which party would you ascribe which position? The NDP for abolition, the Tories and Liberals against? Seems reasonable. But let's look at the reality. Bob Rae, from the only party to long oppose patronage retirement villas, became the would-be saviour of a madeover Senate.

Meanwhile, in the Ontario Legislature, a Conservative MLA, supported by the Liberals, put forward a motion to abolish the Senate. If the Conservatives had won the last twirl of the chairs, doubtless they'd busy themselves saving the Senate, while the NDP in opposition would lead the charge against it. Or, if the PC who moved the motion were a federal politician, he'd likely sashay up to the Triple-E bar.

All three parties seem to operate most of the time from an identical basis. The rules are simple: in power, do approximately what the most powerful want. (Although, given intracorporate contradictions, such as prevailed over the Free Trade Agreement, governments cannot please all of them all the time.) And, in opposition, say what the electorate wants to hear. Watching the political chameleons at work evokes the good cop/bad cop routine. The two try to convince the alleged con that one of them sides with him and the other against. In fact, both cops are on the same team, but playing two different positions. And since they share the same goal, the two can easily switch into either role.

Likewise, the three political parties take up different team positions determined by which side of the throne they occupy. Then they present themselves to the public as opponents. To prove they work for competing teams, they scream their lungs out at each other, sling slurs, hurl moral invective, throw tantrums and storm indignantly from the legislative houses. So offensive is the sandbox spectacle that it embarrasses people watching it on TV! Who, pray tell, other than a fundamentalist preacher, is more righteous than an opposition politician? And who, pray tell, is more compromising than one in power?

Within this ethically bankrupt model—which tends to corrupt even honourable individuals who somehow stumble into politics —how will we ever overcome the mounting crises ruining the country? And if we don't soon come up with a better design, what chance have we of staving off total absorption by our imperialistic neighbours?

THE SURGE IN foodbanks and the ever-growing mass of pavement-dwellers on the doorstep of Canada's riches epitomize most crassly this country's direction and deterioration. They represent how far the magnates will go to lock down their wealth and positions. From their perches on high, no sacrifices are too great for the plebs on low to bear. Officials treat hunger and homelessness with disregard, as if they were innocuous blips not worthy of a big fuss. Indifference to the much-heightened suffering engendered by economic and social policies confirms what has long been evident: the rule of private profit is immune to the concerns of morality.

Despite official disinterest, hunger is a profound problem, deeply symbolic of the growing disenfranchisement and dispossession of Canadians. The march of poverty now encroaches on almost everyone's sense of security. And not only is poverty rising rapidly, but the degree of misery is sinking quickly. Canada has more people at risk of poverty, more already poor, and the poor are poorer than any time since the 1930s.

In *How the Other Half Dies*, author Susan George argues that hunger is no mystery—it's caused by "identifiable forces within the province of rational, human control." Hunger, unlike AIDS, can be cured, the problem solved within the realm of existing knowledge. But does this mean it will be remedied? George explains that it won't, because the remedy would "interfere with someone else's power or profits—locally, nationally or internationally."

Governments in both industrial and developing nations protect "not the right to food but those who violate the right to food," as she puts it in *Ill Fares the Land*, another of her books on world hunger. "The rights of property always supersede the right to eat." That verity stands proud in Canada today as politicians, prodded on by the propertied, hand over public roles to private charities. Foodbanks may be politically sticky, but overall they fill the political bill. Although in a very crude way, foodbanks solve a lot of problems. They take some of the pressure off government cutbacks. They economize on corporate management of waste. They provide a balm for conscience, for a public hankering for social justice but instead held back by a charity straitjacket.

A few foodbanking critics favour scotching what they dub a diversionary venture. Other critics say that if foodbankers genuinely wanted change, not charity, they would do more than dish out food and dabble in self-help. They would adopt Jonathan Kozol's stance. He says activists ought to regard their field, or their workplace, as the lever of change.

It's a notion worth heeding. Foodbankers occupy a unique position *vis-à-vis* the dispossessed. They could no doubt use it to better advantage in combatting poverty. And unless they increase their vigilance, their industry is destined to take part in a U.S.-style welfare disaster. Indeed, foodbankers have good reason to fear that even without their complicity, institutionalized begging as part of a slipshod social net lies ahead. It lies ahead if the top brass get its way.

But the challenge of stemming that danger extends far beyond foodbank and anti-poverty circles. The battle against want can only be won in a broadbased struggle for popular democracy. And were such a democracy to exist, the poor would no longer be forced to subsist on leftovers from the rich.

# Acknowledgements

FRENETIC FOODBANKERS FROM Halifax to Vancouver generously shared their views. They shepherded me through warehouses and from depot to depot. They introduced me to volunteers, to foodbank customers, and to their counterparts in other cities. They loaded me down with clippings and studies. And they generally went out of their way to help.

My heartfelt thanks to everyone who contributed. I am beholden to staff and volunteers in foodbank offices for innumerable favours. As well, my gratitude extends to the many people on both sides of the breadlines I met casually and spoke with briefly. Some of their passing comments made lasting impressions. While more people deserve mention, I list here only those foodbankers and anti-poverty activists formally interviewed.

In Halifax: Dianne Swinemar, executive director, Metro Food Bank Society, and Geoff Regan, boardmember; Joan Mendes, coordinator, Parent Resource Centre (PRC); Carol Desmond, also associated with the PRC and a former volunteer at a local food program; Doug MacDonald, executive director, Ward Five Community Centre.

In New Brunswick: Carolyn McNulty, executive director, Romero House soup kitchen in Saint John; Mike Gendron, executive director, Bathurst Volunteer Centre.

In Montreal: Pierre Legault, founding director of Moisson Montreal; John Pasquini, current Moisson manger; Andrée Ménard, director of Promis (for refugees and immigrants), and Eileen Sheridan, coordinator of community kitchens; Gisèle LeBlanc, director of Garde-Manger (*pour tous*); John Kinloch, coordinator of

Multi Caf community cafeteria and national spokesperson for the Canadian Association of Food Banks (CAFB).

In Ontario: Gerard Kennedy, executive director, Daily Bread Food Bank, Toronto; Lise Corbeil, executive director, Ottawa-based National Anti-Poverty Organization; Joan Turbitt, organizer, Community Unity food and resource bank in Burlington; Glen Pearson, executive director of the London foodbank, and chairperson of the Ontario Association of Food Banks.

In Regina: Ed Bloos, general manager, Regina and District Food Bank, and Eldon Anderson, board chairman; Norma-Jean Dubray-Byrd, project manager, Circle Project; Lorelee Manning, executive director, Council on Social Development; Heather Stevenson, food services coordinator, Food for Learning, and Lil McLean on the board; Carol Kydd, Carmichael United Church emergency food program.

In Edmonton: Marjorie Bencz, executive director, Edmonton Gleaners Association, and Janet Hughes, first president and long-time boardmember, along with Tim Hartnagel, also on the board; Violet Williams, former volunteer for Humans on Welfare and for the foodbank; Christine Bengston, foodbank volunteer.

In British Columbia: Jill van Dijk, executive director, the Vancouver Food Bank, and Lillith Walker, director of advocacy, as well as Sandra Caulien, former foodbank customer, now administrative assistant; Bettina Ptolemy and Art Trovato, volunteers, depot 7 in Vancouver for single parents, and Helga Kanjo, a "client-volunteer" who started Vancouver's first community kitchen; Doug Sabourin, executive director, Association of Neighbourhood Houses, who also serves on the foodbank board; Jean Swanson, executive director, End Legislated Poverty; Fran McDougall, coordinator, Matsqui-Abbotsford Food Bank/Christmas Bureau; Phil Byrne, veteran foodbanker, White Rock.

In addition, my thanks to David Northcott, executive director of the Winnipeg Food Bank, and chairperson of the Canadian Association of Food Banks. Both he and CAFB executive director Barry Davidson provided useful comments on a draft of chapters V and VI.

I am indebted to the work of others for their influence on my views as expressed in *Food for Thought*. In particular: Susan George, for her books on world hunger; Graham Riches, for his writings on hunger and foodbanks in Canada; Hardial Bains for his writings on political economy, and Jonathan Kozol, for many ideas, and for the uncompromising spirit of resistance that imbues his books and inspires me.

Thanks also to Bruce Powe for encouraging me to write for Coach House Press's *Hooligans* series, and for introducing me to Margaret McClintock, Coach House publisher. To Margaret, the Coach House crew and editor David McFadden for being such a pleasure to work with. To Larry Bruner, for telling me parts of my first draft were duds. To Jeffrey Goodman and Valerie MacIntosh for clipping newspapers. To Ilana Yuditsky for assisting with library research.

Special thanks to Chetan Rajani, my muse in a way. And to dear friend Nina Docherty, who, despite a summer of chemotherapy and general hell, worried whether I'd make my deadline.

I am grateful, as always, to my wonderful circle of friends, and to my family, Webbers and Carters both, for providing the psychological cushion that supports me in my life and in my work. Thanks especially to my parents, Ethel and Harvey Webber. And, above all, to David Carter, my mate, best buddy and sounding board.

# Bibliography

*The following is a list of books referred to in the text—*

Barlow, Maude. *Parcel of Rogues: How Free Trade is Failing Canada* (Toronto: Key Porter, 1990).

Conway, John F. *The Canadian Family in Crisis* (Toronto: Lorimer, 1990).

Galbraith, John Kenneth. *The Culture of Contentment* (New York: Houghton Mifflin, 1992).

George, Susan. *Ill Fares the Land: Essays on Food, Hunger and Power* (Washington, D.C.: Institute for Policy Studies, 1984).

———. *How the Other Half Dies: The Real Reasons for World Hunger* (New York: Penguin, 1976).

Guest, Dennis. *The Emergence of Social Security in Canada* (Vancouver: University of British Columbia, 1985).

Hurtig, Mel. *The Betrayal of Canada* (Don Mills: Stoddart, 1991).

McQuaig, Linda. *The Quick and the Dead: Brian Mulroney, Big Business and the Seduction of Canada* (Toronto: Viking, 1991).

Mettrick, Alan. *Last in Line: On the Road and Out of Work—A Desperate Journey with Canada's Unemployed* (Toronto: Key Porter, 1985).

Phillips, Kevin. *The Politics of Rich and Poor: Wealth and the American Electorate in the Reagan Aftermath* (New York: Random House, 1990).

Riches, Graham. *Food Banks and the Welfare Crisis* (Ottawa: Canadian Council on Social Development, 1986).